THE BARBUTO COOKBOOK

The Barbuto Cookbook

CALIFORNIA-ITALIAN COOKING FROM
THE BELOVED WEST VILLAGE RESTAURANT

JONATHAN WAXMAN

FOREWORD BY MARCUS SAMUELSSON

ABRAMS, NEW YORK

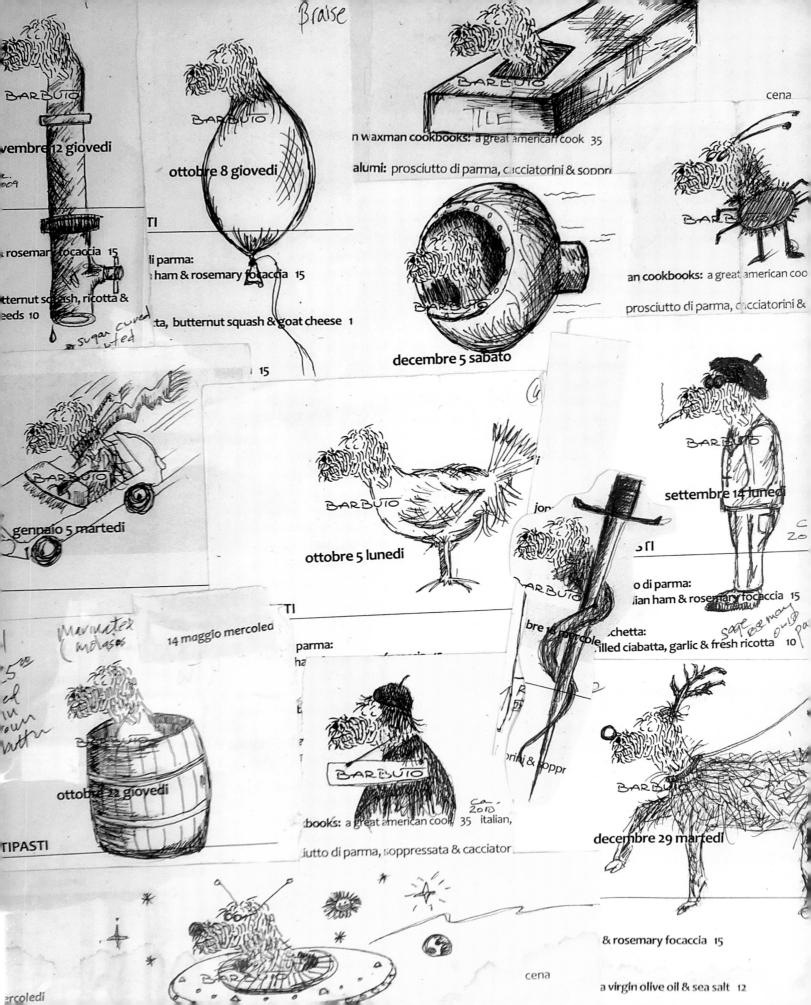

CONTENTS

FOREWORD BY MARCUS SAMUELSSON 7

INTRODUCTION 13

PIZZE 26

ANTIPASTI Includes soups! 46

SALADS 92

PRIMI ~ PASTA, RISOTTO AND GRAINS 116

FISH AND SEAFOOD 158

POULTRY 186

CARNE 200

CONTORNI ~ VEGETABLES 224

SAUCES, OILS, AND PESTOS 248

COCKTAILS 252

PASTRY 260

ACKNOWLEDGMENTS 307

INDEX 313

FOREWORD

When I came to New York in the 1990s as a young cook, Food Network was just starting, and the next generation after Jacques Pépin was emerging. There were new celebrity chefs, and Jonathan Waxman was the coolest of them all. He was cooking for John McEnroe, and all these famous people. He was cooking asparagus, chicken, dumplings, duck, the best food highs you can think of. He was the chef with the blue Ferrari. And we're still chasing that blue Ferrari.

Jonathan is the embodiment of an American chef. He comes from an artistic background—he didn't start out only in food, as the European chefs do. He brings a mix of California and New York, and Europe, too. He is an amazing friend and father. And when I think about Jonathan as an American chef, I think how he brings rock and roll with a touch of jazz to his food.

There's a kindness and warmth around him. You can have a conversation about anything at all, and it will eventually come around to food. You can ask Jonathan about what it was like when California Cuisine emerged, what the food at Michael's was like in the late seventies and early eighties, cooking that still informs American cuisine today. And Jonathan can tell you all about it, because he was *in* it. He was one of the first to look at California Cuisine in the same way we view the food of Paris, and he is comfortable in both those worlds.

You can talk to Jonathan about London, where he has worked extensively with wines. When I opened there a number of years ago, the first person I asked for advice was Jonathan. He connected me to incredible people, and he set me up to feel comfortable in London.

Jonathan can talk with Thomas Keller or Ruth Reichl with equal ease. When you go to an event with him, everyone comes up to hug him. You learn a lot by how people are greeted. Whether it's Nancy Silverton or Jess Shadbolt, Clare de Boer, and Annie Shi, the young British chefs who have opened King in New York City; or Justin Smillie from Upland; they all greet Jonathan as a close friend.

Another thing I love about Jonathan is his love for his family. To be a chef is to be away a lot. We talk about that on the road. He talks about his kids, his family. It's so hard to do what we do, while it's also a privilege. I love when Jonathan tells me about his kids, because I know how hard he works and how much he misses dinners with them. And I can't tell you how many restaurant kids Jonathan has—those he has raised in the industry. Ask Bobby Flay or Aarón Sánchez who comes to mind when they think about their mentor. It's Jonathan. The blue Ferrari seems small compared with all that.

I see Jonathan Waxman and I envision an incredible picnic, with dozens of chefs and food lovers, people who speak the language of food, gathered together. That's what he created in Barbuto. No borders, not New York, or Paris, or Rome, just great food and the people who are drawn to it.

It's the restaurant where we all want to sit and eat gnocchi with asparagus and peas, and roasted chicken. It's got comfort and finesse, warmth, and obvious compassion—and I'm not only talking about the chef. You see it in the dishwashers and the servers, the cooks on the line, the people who are so vital to this industry. And many of them have been at Barbuto since the beginning. Just think for a moment about Luis Ruiz, who started as a dishwasher at Jonathan's restaurant Washington Park twenty years ago and is a trusted lead cook at Barbuto today.

Jonathan exemplifies what it means to be a chef, just as Barbuto embodies what the word restaurant means: to restore the body and the community. It's a place where we come to see one another, to walk table to table. I recall those last days at the original location; there was so much warmth and familiarity. There's no passport. Race, sexuality, religion don't matter. It's just about people. My restaurant, the Red Rooster in Harlem, is an uptown version of that for me. That's why I started in this business. To be able to walk around and sit and talk to people. To find old friends and also to learn something new.

A great restaurant takes on the personality of its owner. You want to be in on whatever they're talking about; you want to taste the food. With Barbuto, Jonathan created that reality down on Washington Street. But there's something else: a great chef and a great restaurant have that je ne sais quoi, an indescribable quality that is largely up to the people who come to dine. It might be crazy, fun, delicious, comforting, a wide range of experiences. It's like an Almodóvar film, or great theater—it's just got that *thing*, and if you could write it down, or turn it into a formula, the restaurant might be done.

I've experienced it myself—my wife and I have ducked into Barbuto on a rainy day, or gone to a photo exhibit upstairs. I've been there on a chef's night out with my chef buddies, all these different experiences that make it a welcoming place and a great watering hole.

The food at Barbuto has that American rock-and-roll quality; it's light and bright, not fussy, but has really good technique. For example, the way he deep-roasts his gnocchi. If you don't roast it in a hot pan, you don't get that crust. And he starts with frozen gnocchi, to help form that crust. He also relies heavily on the farmer's market for ingredients. I've gone with him. It's amazing; he knows all the purveyors, knows their stories. It's different from buying in a store. The menu at Barbuto exists because of the farmer's market.

Jonathan is part of a group of people who are the reason I started in food. I think of Leah Chase, Jonathan Gold, and Anthony Bourdain—people who have so much knowledge; they're great storytellers, and they make experience come alive. Jonathan Waxman is in that group. I long to sit at the table and just have dinner with them all. Last year, I went out for dinner in Los Angeles with Jonathan and Chef Nyesha Arrington. Within the first two minutes of our meal, Jonathan was already deep into sharing one of his restaurant stories. Nyesha and I looked at each other and started laughing. These are really people stories, and Jonathan will never stop telling them.

I don't know what the future will bring. I can't predict when we'll be eating out as we used to. But I do know that we *need* restaurants in order to heal. We need to see one another. We need to hug one another. Cooks need to be mentored, bartenders need to have conversations and pour great wines, and servers need restaurants, even if just as a bridge to the next Broadway play. We need to be seen, need to break bread with one another. I can't wait to have that restorative meal at Barbuto. In the meantime, thanks to the book you are holding, you can create a little bit of that magic yourself at home.

Marcus Samuelsson

THIS BOOK IS DEDICATED TO MY COHORT
IN LIFE, FOOD, AND WINE CRAIG SCHIFFER.
HE WAS THE YANG TO MY YIN.

INTRODUCTION

The West Village restaurant Barbuto has long been a gathering spot for the neighborhood. It has served as a watering hole for locals, knowledgeable New Yorkers, and visitors from all over—a place where the cares of the day-to-day disappear. In its original Washington Street location, it was truly a West Village staple, and, as of this writing, it is well on its way to earning that status again in its new home at 113 Horatio Street, a mere three hundred steps from the original.

Not a day goes by without someone asking me, "What makes Barbuto special?" And the true answer is that I really don't have a clue. In days past, restaurants relied on location, location, and location. Well that is not really a good explanation for Barbuto. When it first opened, the area was seedy and, honestly, scary at night. It hadn't evolved into the trendy neighborhood that it is now.

There were unsavory characters, addicts, and, in winter, a quiet destitution. I had lived in the neighborhood previously for a brief period in the early 1980s, and it hadn't changed much in twenty years. What evolved in a relatively short period of time, between 2003 and

2008, is nothing short of remarkable. Some folks claim that the renovated and gentrified meat market transformed the West Village, for better and worse. Once the blood and guts had departed (for the most part, a few, stubborn, mainly Italian stalwarts remain) then it was a natural migration west. Barbuto opened in this somewhat unstable environment. Soon the social landscape would change.

One of the true game-changing developments was the Standard Hotel. This was a pivotal moment. André Balazs's audacious cement-and-glass edifice over the High Line was truly magnificent. That he convinced the neighbors, planners, and city officials to allow him to build this structure is really something.

After André came more developers, bold architects, dandy visionaries who began to see the potential of this little part of Manhattan. Another brick in the evolutionary wall was the re-creation of the High Line itself. The seemingly unusable rail line that ran adjacent to Barbuto had become a cause célèbre in the West Village. The vast capital spent, the nerve enlisted, and the sheer guts of the visionaries who saw huge potential in a rotting, overhead railway leftover from the early twentieth century—it was nothing short of a miracle. The High Line was really the final set piece needed to change the 'hood. In some ways, Barbuto was an integral part of this history.

Barbuto had a humble beginning.

I never gave it much of a chance, yet in 2003, after I was kicked out of my restaurant Washington Park, I needed income. So, in February 2004, Lynn McNeely and I opened my humble café. The premise of any new restaurant is tied to many notions: the vibe of a building, the competing nearby restaurants, maybe input from a landlord. I truly had no idea what Barbuto would become.

In fact, the name "Barbuto" was an afterthought. My new partner, Fabrizio Ferri, a noble Italian photographer who convinced me to open in his studio, Industria, suggested I do an Italian food joint. I really had no clue what he meant. But his very stubborn and mesmerizing nature forced my hand. We decided to call the restaurant Barbuto, which means "bearded" in Italian. I had a beard, as did Fabrizio, and, most importantly, as did Gideon, Fabrizio's Irish wolfhound.

Fabrizio said I cooked Italian, though my background suggested otherwise. He said my food reminded him of his grandmothers'; simple, and from the heart. He was flattering and persuasive, and he convinced me that maybe an Italian menu was within my grasp.

It is true I had spent many days in Italy, starting in the 1977. I had visited Portofino, Piedmont, and the Val d'Aosta, and I had glimpsed something special there. My California roots were really influenced by Italian food. San Francisco was famous for a certain type of Italian cooking, originating from the Ligurian coast. I had some Italian training. The amazing Mauro Vincente, who owned the terrific REX in downtown LA in the 1980s, tutored me in all things Italian. The inimitable Piero Selvaggio indoctrinated me as well. Piero's Valentino set a very high benchmark for Italian food in America way back in the early 1970s; he was a true pioneer of the new Italian spirit.

When I arrived in New York, in 1983, I began to study and taste food from many Italian restaurants, including Lidia Bastianich's Felidia, Tony May's San Domenico, Da Umberto, Palio, and many other great New York institutions. One very one rainy winter night at Harry's Bar in Venice, in 1980, a brief encounter with Arrigo Cipriani made an indelible impression upon me. And a later sojourn in Venice with Alice Waters bolstered Arrigo's spirit. Another trip to Tuscany ten years later (again with Alice) cemented my love for everything Italian.

It is true I have always loved pasta, risotto, and truffles; and on our honeymoon, my wife Sally and I had spent time in Assisi, Florence, and Verona. And there was Milan. Boy, I loved that town! My traveling buddy, Mark Williamson, who is as intrepid as they come, helped me discover the great sophistication of Milan, the Lago di Como, and Emilia-Romagna.

The week of my fortieth birthday, after stuffing my face in France and Switzerland, I went to Venice, and then Bologna. The trip culminated with a week in Alba. That week, spent tasting for the Tre Bicchieri Italian wine tour, I fell head over heels for the food of Piedmont. White truffles are the stars in the month of November, and the wines of Barolo and Barbaresco make for spectacular menus, but the little farmhouse restaurants in the countryside exude a charm and magic perhaps unparalleled in my experience.

So yes, I had my Italian influences. I had not spent years at Italian grandmothers' stoves, but I have always been a good observer, and these experiences were indelibly etched in my culinary lexicon.

When Lynn and I started Barbuto, we decided to keep it simple. The truth is, I had never made money in the restaurant business. So, I started out with a question: how could I effect a change in my restaurant behavior that might bring about a viable success? I came up with the following:

First: Spend no money on anything other than the essentials.

Second: Limit everything to threes—three types of glassware, a knife, a spoon, and a fork, no menu item that had more than three key ingredients, etc.

Third: No POS system, no managers (this was really dumb, by the way!)

Fourth: Do all the work, don't delegate anything! (Also dumb!)

Fifth: Keep out the froufrou—no tablecloths, no fancy wine lists, no extra items that cost something and add nothing.

Sixth: Spend zero on décor—no lipstick on our pig!

Seventh: Use only dried pasta—it was cheaper, tasted better, held heat longer, and was even more toothsome. (This would change over time, and we would introduce some handmade pastas.)

Eighth: Keep the menu short and sweet—six starters, three pastas, five main courses, and so on.

Ninth: Serve no vegetables with the main courses; let the customer dictate what to order to accompany their meal.

Tenth: Have many affordable wines by the glass.

Eleventh: Nothing should cost more than nineteen dollars! (This last edict pissed off all my colleagues.)

Voilà—Barbuto was born! Not to great fanfare, however. The *New York Times* called me a phantom (I liked the notorious quality of the jibe!). True to plan, we hired no manager (this was really stupid!). But we became very busy, truly in spite of ourselves.

I did have a trick up my sleeve. We opened with a conventional gas grill. Three months later, my preordered double-decker pizza oven and grill arrived. Built by the extremely talented and elusive Nobile Attie, the oven is a masterpiece, a beast and a bear to learn.

With the addition of this magnificent oven, Barbuto was elevated in a culinary sense to a new playing field. Suddenly we could handle the massive volume, and the oven's warm fire charmed the customers and created an environment in the kitchen that gave the whole place a special quality.

From the beginning I designed the menu to be fairly static. We would always feature a salumi platter, a chicken plate, a fish, and meat. The mystique of Barbuto, then, is slightly complicated—I suppose like any successful restaurant. I have had some extraordinary chefs in fifteen years: Lynn McNeely; Heather Miller; Justin Smillie; Andrew Curren; Roel Alcudia; Melissa Lopez; Travis McShane; and present day—Josh Stumbaugh. Pastry has always been the domain of Heather Miller—she is extraordinary and patient, and most brilliant! These great chefs have been the backbone of Barbuto.

A terrific restaurant can't exist without a captain. That person is the former ballerina Jen Davidson. Jen has devoted fifteen years to Barbuto and me. Her influence is indelible and extraordinary. She is an irreplaceable individual; she is the heartbeat of Barbuto. Jen is tough, stubborn, and funny. She is dedicated, smart, and passionate. She is my restaurant wife, and we finish each other's sentences.

The other player in our little drama is my wine director, Michael Kelly. He was there at the beginning. He did leave after a few years as our bartender extraordinaire, but he came back for more punishment. He has evolved into a master sommelier, completely without pretention.

My chefs, with of course the brilliant team of Jen and Michael, are the essence, the magic, and the pulse of Barbuto. All these great employees (really, my family!) have collaborated to help me create hundreds of recipes. In this book I have selected more than 150 of the best recipes gleaned from that collaboration.

The recipes are divided along the major food groups we serve at Barbuto: soups, salads, pizzas, hot appetizers, cold starters, salumi, primi (pasta, risottos, and grains), fish and seafood, poultry, meats, vegetables, desserts, and cocktails.

The recipes wander across Italy, Europe, and the United States. I wanted to portray the recipes in their true form, exactly as we do them at the restaurant. You will find them to be uncomplicated, and they use many readily available foods. If your local butcher does not have pancetta, I offer an alternative. If you want to make a clam dish and the clams are not up to snuff, I will suggest a viable substitute.

And at long last, how to answer that question of what makes Barbuto special? There are many factors. Where did the magic come from? How did we bottle it? And how do we dispense it? My staff has a unique perspective. They *know* where the bottle of Barbuto magic is. This bottle contains the magic: the Barbuto chicken, the Barbuto vibe, the amazing West Village location, and the purity of the kale salad. The bottle is not hard to top off, because my staff provides the ingredients. They know the Barbuto way of keeping things simple. They also know that a restaurant is a restorative place. They are the custodians of that restorative power. My cooks laugh while they work. Can that be true? Yes, because at Barbuto we value empathy and civility. At the end of the day, I just want to throw a big party every night. And I want you to join.

Barbuto's original location in a garage with giant garage doors proved to be a huge asset, not the opposite. Our new space, in the 1898 building of a former ice manufacturer, has a similar vibe. Perhaps not that of a garage, but close. The best thing about the new space is its size. At Barbuto, while we adored the space, it truly was not big enough or robust enough for the crowds we accommodated. These folks now won't have far to travel, and the menu will be very familiar, as will the wine list.

For all of you at home, I invite you into our little world. We will give you the tools to make Barbuto classics and I will instruct you in the ways to make cooking fun! We will talk seasonality, freshness, and, most importantly, editing ourselves. It will become quickly apparent that Barbuto food is decidedly easy to make—two or three ingredients turn into a soul-satisfying meal.

We believe in elevating basic foods like zucchini and tomatoes into transformative recipes that are short and concise. You will find pasta dishes that have lemon, garlic, and butter and yet lack for nothing. You will discover how much fun you can have making pizza dough and topping it with a surprising array of ingredients. I want you to spend your time loving to cook and eager to sample your creations. That's the Barbuto way!

PIZZE

PIZZA WAS ALWAYS ON MY MIND when I first opened Barbuto. The special oven that the very talented Nobile Attie and I designed was created to include both a grill and a pizza oven in a single unit. It is an oven that my colleagues covet and are truly fascinated by. Our grill chef at Barbuto needs to be deft and skilled to the point where they can perform the tasks of two people. The Nobile-Waxman oven is that good!

As far as inspiration goes; well, I have had superb pizzas the world over. My first Italian pizza was in the Milan train station in 1977. It came from a wood-oven pizza vendor located inside the main train station. The taste of that pizza was a shock to my system. This pizza had nothing to do with the pizza of my youth. First of all, it was a personal-sized pizza, not meant for sharing. The fire had imparted a charred flavor, and the perfume wafting up from the bubbling hot cheese and tomato topping was intoxicating.

I had spent years eating pizza in Berkeley at Giovanni's Pizzeria on Shattuck Avenue (cooked by a very nice Chinese fellow). In my rock-and-roll years, I consumed many a late-night pie at Lavelle's, a Berkeley standby where my band, Dixie Peach, would play five long sets before we consumed massive, palate-burning pepperoni pizzas at three in the morning, washed down with cheap pilsner.

I also loved the pizza at Lombardi's in San Francisco, where I remember a calzone with a creamy, thyme-flavored, goat cheese filling. While I was attending cooking school in Paris in the mid-1970s, French pizza was not a great option, but there were a few choices on the Left Bank that featured small pies with good ingredients. The first pizza that I can refer to as a California pizza was at the café in Chez Panisse, where the amazing pizzaiolo Michele Perrella would very deliberately cook delicious, small, hand-crafted pizzas. They were crusty, bursting with a nutty, smoky crispness. He would top them with perfect ingredients; not too many, nor too few.

And then my dear friend and fellow chef Wolfgang Puck lifted the Chez Panisse ideal and made it his own. His signature pie of smoked salmon on crème fraîche with caviar at his revolutionary Spago was a revelation, and certainly not traditional!

These memories lingered with me as I was designing the teeny kitchen at Barbuto in 2003. And then Nobile Attie and I devised the formidable and lovely double-decker oven-grill. One of the main features was a true dome-roofed pizza oven. It did work wonders on pizzas, and we thought we had the magic formula. But my best-laid plans did not foresee the blessed and cursed problem of sheer volume.

At dinner service it became readily apparent that the pizza oven would have to be used to cook my signature chickens. So, the pizza oven morphed into a chicken oven! We devised a decent compromise, to comply with my desire to serve pizza. Back in 2004, dinners were booming, but our lunches were slow. I then decided that my oven might be able to handle both chickens and perhaps a couple of pizzas; but solely at lunchtime. That worked superbly, until things picked up, and lunch got off the hook!

Then a small miracle happened. We had a very clever dishwasher turned line cook named Luis Ruiz, who was able to master the trick of cooking pizzas, steaks, fish, and chicken simultaneously in that crazy oven and never miss a beat. Luis's acumen and boldness allowed us to serve pizza at lunch and brunch. The only downside was the occasional request for pizza at dinner; we just shrugged and told them to please come back for lunch.

PIZZA DOUGH

MAKES FOUR
8-OUNCE (225 G)
DOUGH BALLS

1 cup (240 ml) Biga, thawed
    if frozen (recipe below)
1½ cups (360 ml) purified
    water at 100°F (38°C),
    plus more as needed
6 tablespoons (90 ml) olive oil
1 teaspoon sea salt
½ cup (120 g) organic whole-
    wheat flour
2½ cups (320 g) organic
    all-purpose flour, plus
    2 tablespoons for the
    counter and more for
    dusting
1 envelope (2¼ teaspoons)
    active dry yeast

Originally, we tried two different versions of pizza dough. One appeared in *Italian My Way*. That recipe utilized beer, honey, and commercial yeast. The current Barbuto version is presented here. There are a couple of ways to procure a biga: ask for a cup from your local baker, or make your own.

1 In a large bowl, mix the biga with the water, oil, salt, and both flours. Add the yeast.

2 Gently mix together with your hands until everything is just incorporated, adding more water if it looks too dry—it should be a soft and slightly sticky dough. Let sit, covered, for 2 hours, or until doubled in size. Punch the dough down and add the all-purpose flour.

3 Cover with a clean tea towel and let sit for 3 hours or until doubled in size.

4 Flour a tabletop or counter with 2 tablespoons flour. Cut into four 8-ounce (225 g) portions. Form into balls and then dust with flour and refrigerate for 2 hours. The dough is ready to use in any of the recipes that follow; it will rise in the cold, and that is okay.

Biga

1 envelope (2¼ teaspoons)
    active dry yeast
2 tablespoons olive oil
1 cup (235 ml) warm water,
    plus more if necessary
1 cup (120 g) organic all-
    purpose flour

1   Mix the yeast with the oil and water. Let sit for 30 minutes.

2   Put the flour in the bowl of a stand mixer with the dough hook. On low speed, add the water-yeast mixture slowly, mixing until incorporated.

3   Add more water to achieve a supple and tender dough. The moisture of the dough will depend on the weather that day—more or less humidity will determine how much water you may need to add.

4   Scoop the biga into an oiled bowl and let rest for 2 hours. It will rise to double in size.

5   Punch down and use right away or freeze in 1-cup (240 ml) portions.

PIZZA UOVO

baked farm eggs, ricotta, and pancetta

MAKES 2 PIZZAS (ENOUGH FOR 8 PEOPLE)

2 tablespoons olive oil
16 ounces (450 g) Pizza
    Dough (page 30), divided
    in half
2 tablespoons green garlic oil
Sea salt
½ cup (115 g) diced pancetta
    (thick-cut bacon will do)
4 ounces (115 g) ricotta
3 ounces (55 g) fontina cheese
2 eggs, cracked into a bowl
1 ounce grated Parmesan
    cheese

I don't like to admit it, but I have issues with eggs. A child-hood issue—no one is perfect! However, a majority of my customers love eggs, especially on pizza! So, bowing to public demand, I succumbed to capitalism and started serving egg-topped pizza.

How to cook the egg(s)? I suggest breaking them into small separate dishes that barely contain the eggs. Then upend each dish near the middle of the pie. Gently, but with a firm hand, return the pie to the oven. Wait a minute, and then turn the pie 90 degrees. Turn one more time and in about 3 to 4 minutes the egg will be set and the pie is done.

1   Preheat the oven to 450°F (230°C) on convection setting, if available, for about an hour. Oil two round pizza trays (a regular baking sheet is okay too) with the oil.

2   Spread the dough on the pizza trays (half on each tray) and then slather with the green garlic oil and sprinkle with salt. Sprinkle the pancetta over the two rounds of dough.

3   Dot with the ricotta and fontina, dividing evenly between the two pizzas.

4   Bake for 3 minutes. Pull out the pizza and set on the stove top.

5   Then gently pour one egg onto the middle of each pizza; return to the oven and bake until the eggs are set (about 4 minutes).

6   Remove pizzas from oven and sprinkle with the Parmesan. Cut into squares and serve.

CLAM PIZZA

new potatoes, crème fraîche, and Parmesan

**MAKES 2 PIZZAS
(ENOUGH FOR
8 PEOPLE)**

1 cup (125 g) fingerling
   potatoes
5 tablespoons olive oil, divided
Sea salt
16 ounces (450 g) Pizza
   Dough (page 30), divided
   in half
1 cup (125 g) freshly shucked
   clams (if not available, a
   good substitution is rock
   shrimp)
1 clove garlic, minced
2 tablespoons grated
   Parmesan cheese
2 tablespoons crème fraîche

This is an homage to the famous Pepe's in East Haven, Connecticut. The person who introduced me to Pepe's was my dear buddy Jeff Salaway, a fellow gastronome and intrepid eater. Jeff and I had many things in common. But our number-one passion was Italian food. We tried to eat at Pepe's one night and they were full, so we ate in the annex. The huge pie was lightly burned, with extremely fresh chopped clams, garlic, and Parmesan. It was ethereal, a real vision of pizza. Here is my version.

1   Bring a pot of salted water to a simmer, add the potatoes, and cook until tender, about 35 minutes. Remove the potatoes from the water and let cool on a kitchen towel.

2   When the potatoes are cool, slice them and toss them with 2 tablespoons of the oil. Lightly season with salt.

3   Preheat the oven to 450°F (230°C) on convection setting, if available, for about an hour. Oil two round pizza trays (a regular baking sheet is okay too) with 2 tablespoons oil.

4   Spread the dough on the pizza trays (half on each tray), dimple it, and sprinkle with salt.

5   Toss the clams with the garlic, potatoes, and remaining 1 tablespoon oil.

6   Sprinkle the dough with the clams and the potatoes (half on each pizza), then broadcast the cheese all over.

7   Bake until nice and golden, 10–12 minutes; check that the bottoms are cooked.

8   Remove from the pan and spread the crème fraîche all over (half on each pizza). Cut into rectangles or wedges and serve.

EGGPLANT PIZZA

tomato, ricotta, and parsley

MAKES 2 PIZZAS
(ENOUGH FOR
8 PEOPLE)

2 cups (165 g) diced purple
    eggplant
Sea salt
5 tablespoons olive oil, divided
1 cup (180 g) diced heirloom
    tomatoes
16 ounces (450 g) Pizza
    Dough (page 30), divided
    in half
2 tablespoons burrata cheese
2 tablespoons ricotta
1 tablespoon Parmesan cheese
2 tablespoons chopped fresh
    parsley leaves

A nice way to spend a summer's afternoon. The eggplants should be firm, colorful, and sweet. The tomatoes, bursting with juice and flavor. The ricotta, creamy; and the green parsley garnish light and fresh, not tough.

1   Preheat the oven to 400°F (205°C).

2   In a bowl, toss the eggplant with sea salt and 3 tablespoons of the oil. Place on a sheet pan and roast for 15–20 minutes until tender and eatable.

3   Turn up the oven temperature to 450°F (230°C). Oil two round pizza trays (a regular baking sheet is okay too) with the remaining 2 tablespoons oil.

4   Spread the dough on the pizza trays (half on each tray), dimple it, and sprinkle with salt.

5   Top the dough with half the eggplant and tomatoes (half on each pizza).

6   Dot each pie with half of the burrata, ricotta, and Parmesan, and sprinkle with the parsley.

7   Bake the pizzas until golden brown, 10–12 minutes.

8   Cut into rectangles or wedges and serve.

SWEET POTATO PIZZA

sweet potato, onion, and mozzarella

MAKES 2 PIZZAS (ENOUGH FOR 8 PEOPLE)

½ sweet potato (about 4½ ounces/150 g)
3 tablespoons olive oil, divided
Sea salt
16 ounces (450 g) Pizza Dough (page 30), divided in half
1 tablespoon grated Parmesan cheese, plus more for finishing
½ sweet onion, peeled and thinly sliced
⅓ cup (57 g) chopped bacon
½ cup (65 g) diced mozzarella
1 tablespoon chopped fresh parsley

I love sweet potatoes. They are not generally used on pizza, but they should be! Sweet potatoes are unexpectedly perfect on pizza. Add the sliced onion, mozzarella, and pancetta or bacon, and this is a winning combo.

1   Preheat the oven to 450°F (230°C)

2   Peel the sweet potato and slice into ¼-inch-thick rounds (you should have about 1 cup/145 g). Lay the slices out on a cookie sheet.

3   Sprinkle the sweet potatoes with 1 tablespoon of olive oil and some sea salt.

4   Bake for 20–25 minutes, until tender. Remove and let cool.

5   Oil two round pizza trays (a regular baking sheet is okay too) with the remaining 2 tablespoons oil.

6   Spread the dough on the pizza trays (half on each tray), dimple it, and sprinkle with salt.

7   Sprinkle the dough with the Parmesan, then strategically place the sweet potato, onion, bacon, and finally the mozzarella (half on each pizza).

8   Bake the pizzas until golden brown, 10–12 minutes. Garnish with more Parmesan and the parsley. Cut into rectangles or wedges and serve.

PIZZA BAMBINI

tomato sauce, mozzarella, and basil

SERVES 2 PIZZAS (ENOUGH FOR 8 KIDS)

3 tablespoons olive oil, divided
16 ounces (450 g) Pizza Dough (page 30), divided in half
12 tablespoons (60 ml) Tomato Sauce (page 249)
8 ounces (227 g) mozzarella cheese
4 tablespoons (25 g) grated Parmesan cheese
12 fresh basil leaves

Kids! Barbuto is that place where we have successfully integrated families into the mix. I had always wished for a wide demographic base, including families with kids of all ages. We found a spot to store strollers; we loved when kids used the Industria atrium to play games, and I love watching kids eat!

Kids' menus have always appalled me. They're usually throwaway attempts to placate parents and quiet the little ones. We have worked hard to make any dishes designated *bambini* as delicious for adults as for kids. Here is the classic, a Margarita pizza that has the right amount of sauce, a sturdy dough, the best mozzarella cheese, and a bit of Parmesan—that's it! Everyone loves the simplicity, and we have made a lot of friends with these pies.

1 Preheat the oven to 450°F (230°C) on convection setting, if available, for about an hour. Oil two round pizza trays (a regular baking sheet is okay too) with 2 tablespoons of the oil.

2 Spread the dough on the pizza trays (half on each tray) and sprinkle with the remaining 1 tablespoon oil.

3 Spread the sauce over the dough (half on each pizza), dot with mozzarella, and then sprinkle with the Parmesan.

4 Bake until golden brown, about 10–12 minutes. Cut into rectangles or wedges, garnish with the basil, and serve.

WILD MUSHROOM PIZZA

basil oil and Gruyère

MAKES 2 PIZZAS (ENOUGH FOR 8 PEOPLE)

3 tablespoons olive oil, divided
16 ounces (450 g) Pizza Dough (page 30), divided in half
1 cup (65 g) wild mushrooms, washed and cut in half
2 tablespoons basil oil (page 251)
6 ounces (55 g) grated Gruyère cheese
4 tablespoons (25 g) grated Parmesan cheese
2 tablespoons chopped chives

Mushrooms are great. Most people find them interesting and appealing, and they are very easy to cook, requiring not much more than a bit of olive oil, seasoning, and heat to bring out their flavor. The difference between domestic and wild varieties can really vary. I adore cepes (porcini), chanterelles, morels, and hen of the woods. All these make for great pizzas. However, the lowly cremini mushroom, widely available, can have great charm and flavor if handled correctly. Pay close attention when buying the hothouse varieties; I look for firm flesh, closed caps, and no ammonia odor.

1   Preheat the oven to 450°F (230°C) on convection setting, if available, for about an hour. Oil two round pizza trays (a regular baking sheet is okay too) with 2 tablespoons of the oil.

2   Spread the dough on the pizza trays (half on each tray) and then dimple with your fingertips.

3   Toss the mushrooms with the basil oil. Spread evenly over the dough.

4   Cover the pizzas evenly with both cheeses.

5   Drizzle with the remaining tablespoon olive oil.

6   Bake until golden brown, 10–12 minutes.

7   Garnish with chives, cut into rectangles or wedges, and serve hot.

ASPARAGUS PIZZA

shaved asparagus, prosciutto, and goat cheese

**MAKES 2 PIZZAS
(ENOUGH FOR
8 PEOPLE)**

3 tablespoons olive oil, divided
16 ounces (450 g) pizza dough
  (page 30), divided in half
Flour for dusting
1 cup (225 g) shaved
  asparagus
½ cup julienned prosciutto
2 tablespoons chopped chives
Sea salt
1 cup (240 ml) fresh goat
  cheese (you can substitute
  ricotta)
4 tablespoons (25 g) grated
  Parmesan cheese

Here is a delightful, almost delicate pie. The dough needs to be very thin and cooked quickly. A bit of advice to make this come out well: roll the dough out with a heavy rolling pin, dusting with flour. Then place the dough on your knuckles and gently stretch it. This is the technique for filo dough and other doughs that need to be very thin.

1 Preheat the oven to 450°F (230°C) on convection setting, if available, for about an hour. Oil two round pizza trays (a regular baking sheet is okay too) with 2 tablespoons of the oil.

2 In a bowl, mix the asparagus and prosciutto.

3 Spread the dough on the pizza trays (half on each tray), dimple it, and sprinkle it with salt.

4 Toss the asparagus and prosciutto with the remaining 1 tablespoon oil, the chives, and salt. Spread the asparagus-proscuitto mixture evenly over the dough (half on each pizza).

5 Dot with the goat cheese, and then sprinkle with the Parmesan.

6 Bake until golden brown, 10–12 minutes.

7 Cut into rectangles or wedges and serve hot.

BRUSSELS SPROUT PIZZA

**MAKES 2 PIZZAS
(ENOUGH FOR
8 PEOPLE)**

2 cups (180 g) Brussels
    sprouts, leaves separated
6 tablespoons (60 ml) olive oil
4 tablespoons (25 g) grated
    Parmesan cheese
1 clove garlic, minced
Red chile flakes
16 ounces (450 g) Pizza
    Dough (page 30)
Sea salt
8 tablespoons (55 g) grated
    Manchego cheese

This is a fun idea. Take the leaves of Brussels sprouts, toss them in olive oil, then with red pepper, garlic, and Manchego cheese, and then bake them with fresh tomatoes and thyme. The Brussels sprouts become crisp and succulent, and the pizza is pure pleasure.

1   Toss the Brussels sprouts with 2 tablespoons of the oil, the Parmesan, garlic, and chile.

2   Preheat the oven to 450°F (230°C) on convection setting, if available, for about an hour. Oil two round pizza trays (a regular baking sheet is okay too) with 2 tablespoons of the oil.

3   Spread the dough on the pizza trays (half on each tray), dimple it, and sprinkle it with salt.

4   Sprinkle the dough with 2 tablespoons olive oil and salt.

5   Evenly spread the Brussels sprouts and then the Manchego over the dough (half on each pizza).

6   Bake until golden brown, 10–12 minutes.

7   Cut into squares or wedges and serve hot.

CHORIZO AND KALE PIZZA

MAKES 2 PIZZAS (ENOUGH FOR 8 PEOPLE)

2 tablespoons olive oil

16 ounces (450 g) Pizza Dough (page 30), divided in half

12 tablespoons Tomato Sauce (page 249)

1 cup (450 g) loose chorizo sausage

1 cup (65 g) chopped kale

1 cup (110 g) mozzarella cheese

4 tablespoons (25 g) grated Parmesan cheese

I love these ingredients; I realize that they are unusual, but what the hell! They are fun together and make a terrific pie!

1 Preheat the oven to 450°F (230°C) on a convection, if available, for about an hour. Oil two round pizza trays (a regular baking sheet is okay too) with 2 tablespoons of oil.

2 Spread the dough on the pizza trays (half on each tray).

3 Spread the tomato sauce over the dough (half on each pizza).

4 Dot with the chorizo, kale, and mozzarella.

5 Sprinkle with the Parmesan and bake until golden brown, 10–12 minutes.

6 Cut into rectangles or wedges and serve hot.

BLACK TRUFFLE PIZZA

crème fraîche and chanterelle mushrooms

MAKES 2 PIZZAS (ENOUGH FOR 8 PEOPLE)

4 tablespoons (60 ml) olive oil, divided
16 ounces (450 g) Pizza Dough (page 30), divided in half
Sea salt
1 cup (55 g) washed, dried, and sliced chanterelles
1 shallot, sliced
6 tablespoons crème fraîche
4 tablespoons (25 g) grated Parmesan cheese
1 ounce (28 g) black truffle (summer truffles are just okay)

The truffle is an ideal accompaniment for any pizza. We shave them raw over tomatoes, cheese, sausage, clams, and more. The truffles need to be copious, but an ounce goes a long way. A true companion for the truffles are mushrooms. Many folks confuse mushrooms and truffles; they are both fungi, but truffles are part of the ecology of trees and mushrooms are far more independent, they can exist on rotting logs, damp peat soil, sand, and so on. The close proximity of their mutual growth environments makes them well suited to pairing up. Mixing chanterelles and porcini with truffles is a perfect storm, a marriage of lofty ambitions.

1   Preheat the oven to 450°F (230°C) on convection setting, if possible, for about an hour. Oil two round pizza trays (a regular baking sheet is okay too) with 2 tablespoons of the oil.

2   Spread the dough over the pizza trays (half on each tray), dimple it, and sprinkle it with salt.

3   Sprinkle the dough with the remaining 2 tablespoons oil.

4   Sprinkle with the mushrooms, shallot, crème fraîche, and Parmesan (half on each pizza).

5   Season with salt and bake until golden brown, 10 to 12 minutes.

6   Remove from the oven. Using a truffle slicer, cover both pizzas with truffle slices. Cut into rectangles or wedges and serve hot.

ANTIPASTI

INCLUDES SOUPS!

THE WORD "ANTIPASTO" is quite specific. It means to whet one's appetite, to give our immediate hunger pangs and cravings a base so that the rest of the meal will proceed in a smooth fashion. The traditional starter foods, like salumi (Italian cold cuts, usually made from pork), cheese, roasted peppers, and so on, are all wonderful, but at Barbuto we also include a whole array of bruschette, crostini, and cured vegetables. These will range from the simple to the complex; vegan to meat central.

The mainstay of antipasti is salumi—pork products like speck, culatello, capicola, lonza, guanciale, and prosciutto. And then there is the world of salami. My San Francisco background has provided me with ample opportunity to sample many types of salami, and I generally prefer the medium-cured Genovese but I love them all.

One of the first purchases for Barbuto was an antique Berkel slicer. My Roman partner, Fabrizio Ferri, has a house in Milan. Fabrizio knew of a store in Milan that only sold massive grape scales and antique meat slicers. While there with Fabrizio, I fell in love with a vintage model that resembled a cross between a bathtub and a 1950s Porsche 356.

It was shipped over for the opening. I was showing it off to a buddy one day when he accidently dropped his coffee and knocked the machine to the floor! Luckily there was a Berkel repair guy still working on the Bowery in New York, and he came to our rescue. This wonderful machine, battered and bruised, has lumbered on for fifteen years. I am sure it is totally in need of a tune-up at this juncture!

Barbuto's history with soup is fairly straightforward. It was never intended to be a "classy joint" with fancy soups; we just wanted folks to be happy. In fact, I can't think of an instance where we had a kitchen meeting to explore the subject. Yet soups are the cornerstone of cooking, the mark of a decent cook. That mark can be many things: a good knowledge of cookery through the ages, a rich cookbook collection, a functional kitchen, good knife skills, etcetera . . . but for me, being able to cook the basics is key. At the top of that list is the ability to conjure up a decent soup.

A good soup is neither easy nor hard; it kinda sits in the middle of the room, technique-wise. Some chefs believe soups to be a venue solely for leftovers. On the other hand, I have fancy colleagues who use only the choicest of ingredients—say, wild mushrooms, truffles, or lobster. They adore creating luxurious, beautiful, lush soups. I have no quarrel with a soup of Belon oysters in the guise of an elaborate onion soup; it just ain't Barbuto!

So, I have written some complex soup recipes and a few that are dead simple. I guess I want your soup vocabulary to increase, so feel free to experiment with both.

Barbuto is a happy place, and soup is a happy dish. We are reminded every autumn how important a hot, warming soup can be—the seafood soup I have included is a perfect example of that happy place. Soup has taken a back seat on menus lately, especially in New York City. It is as if the dining public views soup as a fast-casual commodity, best bought on the go from the local bodega. The soup restaurants have displaced soup as well; they specialize in a dish, and that suggests that we don't have to.

But I love and cherish soups: they cure our colds and sore throats, warm us on frigid winter nights, and comfort us at lunch when we most need it.

RIBOLLITA

Butternut squash, kale, leeks, and canned tomato

SERVES 4

3 tablespoons butter
2 cups peeled, seeded, and
 diced futsu or butternut
 squash plus four 1-inch
 (2.5 cm) slices for garnish
Sea salt and freshly ground
 black pepper
1 tablespoon olive oil, plus
 more for the toast
2 onions, diced
2 leeks, tops removed, diced,
 and thoroughly washed
3 cloves garlic, smashed, plus
 1 clove cut in half
2 cups (100 g) chopped kale
1 (8-ounce/225 g) can peeled
 San Marzano tomatoes
4 cups (about 1 L) chicken
 stock
4½ thick slices sourdough
 bread
1 tablespoon chopped fresh
 parsley
1 tablespoon grated Parmesan
 cheese

Ribollita is a delightful brothy concoction that the cooks at Barbuto love to play with. It is an adaptable soup that lends itself well to seasonal cooking, the Barbuto way! It is an extremely satisfying first course—a perfect cold-weather dish, and a colorful one to boot. The futsu squash, a recent Japanese import, has become a very popular squash. It is magnificent: fruity, meaty, with a very nutty flesh and a skin that is edible. If you can't find it, use butternut. This soup contains my absolute favorite ingredient: kale, the foundation of the ribollita.

1   In an enameled casserole on the stovetop, heat 2 tablespoons of butter over medium heat. Add the diced squash, season with salt and pepper, and cook over medium heat until cooked through. Transfer to a bowl and keep warm.

2   In the casserole, add 1 tablespoon olive oil, the remaining 1 tablespoon butter, the onions, leeks, and smashed garlic and cook for 10 minutes. Season with salt and pepper.

3   Add the squash to the onions and cook for 3 minutes.

4   Add the kale, tomatoes, and stock and bring to a boil.

5   Reduce the heat to a murmur and cook for 1 hour, uncovered, or until the broth tastes rich.

6   Toast the slices of bread until very golden. Rub each slice of toast with the halved clove of raw garlic and sprinkle with olive oil.

7   Sprinkle the parsley and cheese over the ribollita and garnish with the squash slices. Serve the garlic-toasted sourdough alongside.

JERUSALEM ARTICHOKE SOUP

peas and carrots

SERVES 4

I never saw or heard of a Jerusalem artichoke until I went to school in Paris. In French the word is quite unique and funny to my ears: *topinambour*! They would appear sporadically in places like Hediard and Fauchon (the ivory tower food halls on the Place Madeleine in Paris). Then one day, all hell broke loose and the stalls were filled with piles of these gorgeous tubers.

While it's nothing like an artichoke (it is sometimes called a sunchoke), the Jerusalem artichoke is an amazing vegetable. It can be nutty, rich, crispy, dense, and light; it dances to many tunes.

When cooked to a puree, it turns fluffy and develops a unique flavor. It has no bitterness like an artichoke, and it is much sweeter. Hence it can caramelize better than a lot of other vegetables. It can be treated much like a carrot. I like them unpeeled, but some people are turned off by the skin. I find that the skin lends an extra note of flavor, and I imagine the skin has many nutrients as well. The tuber is native to the Americas and in fact helped the French survive the long winters in Canada in the seventeenth century. For some reason, they were nearly forgotten in the United States until the 1990s.

I imagine the influence came from France, where Jerusalem artichokes are considered by some to be the best vegetable to make a soup. Which brings me to my

4 tablespoons (55 g) butter
1 pound washed and cubed
  Jerusalem artichokes
1 onion, peeled and diced
1 cup diced carrots
4 cups Vegetable Broth (recipe
  below)
Sea salt and freshly ground
  black pepper
1 cup (145 g) shelled peas
  (frozen is okay)
2 tablespoons Salsa Verde
  (page 250)

soup. All you have to do is wash the tubers to remove any dirt or sand. They need to be cut into rough cubes or slices and then cooked with onions and carrots.

Once they have caramelized, you can add either water or vegetable broth, bring to a boil, then simmer for an hour. Cook the peas and favas separately. I don't mind a bit of roughness in the porridge, so I do not strain them.

1   Heat the butter in a small stockpot over medium heat. Add the Jerusalem artichokes, onion, and carrots. Season them with salt and pepper and cook until golden and tender, about 20 minutes.

2   Add the vegetable broth and bring to a boil. Lower the heat and cook slowly, stirring occasionally, for 1 hour.

3   Using an immersion blender, puree the soup.

4   Cook the peas in boiling water until tender, about 3 to 5 minutes, depending on their size, and add them to the soup. Finally, add the salsa verde. Season with salt and pepper and serve hot.

Vegetable Broth

M A K E S   O N E   Q U A R T

8 ounces white button
  mushrooms, sliced
1 fennel bulb, diced
1 onion, peeled and diced
2 carrots, peeled and diced
3 cloves garlic, peeled and
  sliced
2 tablespoons olive oil
Sea salt and freshly ground
  black pepper

1   In a 4 quart saucepan, add all the ingredients and cook on medium for 10 minutes.

2   Season the vegetables with salt and pepper and add 2 quarts cold water. Bring to a boil, then simmer for 2 hours, covered. Strain and let cool. Discard the vegetables.

ZUPPA DI COZZE

mussels, fennel, and couscous

SERVES 6

1 cup (150 g) Israeli couscous
2 tablespoons olive oil, divided
1 cup diced fennel
1 cup (240 ml) white wine
2 jalapeños, seeded and
    minced
2 pints (450 g) fresh mussels,
    scrubbed and debearded
2 tablespoons butter

I love this soup, and it is substantial enough for a main course. Mussels are sometimes overlooked, and perhaps that is a question of freshness. Locally, we get mussels from Puget Sound, Maine; for years Prince Edward Island mussels were the go-to source.

I like tiny, briny mussels, like the ones from Normandy in France. The bigger mussels are flabby and are not a good choice for this recipe. The mussels you buy should smell like the sea. They should be shiny black, and, more important, their shells need to be tightly shut. I like to rinse them in cold water to remove any excess sand and also to trim out any "beard" you might find protruding from the mussels.

Mussels are incredibly nutritious and devoid of fat. They consist mainly of protein. The recipe calls for Israeli couscous, a whole grain that marries well with the mussels. The fennel will add crunch as well as a note of anise.

1   Cook the couscous in boiling water for 8–10 minutes until al dente. Drain and toss with 1 tablespoon of the olive oil. Keep warm.

2   In a cast-iron skillet, cook the fennel in the remaining 1 tablespoon oil over medium-high heat for 12 to 15 minutes, stirring well. Season with salt and pepper.

3   Add the wine, jalapeños, and mussels, bring to a boil, then cover and steam until the mussels open, 6 to 8 minutes. Discard any mussels that have not opened.

4   Add the couscous and the butter to the mussels and fennel and toss well. Let steam for 5 minutes or until fluffy. Serve hot.

OXTAIL SOUP

spaetzle, autumn vegetables, and savory

SERVES 8

"Oxtail" is such a romantic name. It harkens back to a distant and softer time. I guess to protect butchers from selling pieces of a beef tail, the name "ox" was used, and it has stuck.

Up to that point, butchers probably gave away the oxtail or reserved the best ones for themselves. High in gelatin and fiber, the tail meat makes for fabulous broth. And that is what we are after: a marvelous concoction of rich, beefy broth imbued with the flavor of savory and garnished with carrots, turnips, and celery root. These root vegetables become the stars. They are all high in nutritional goodness and dense umami notes, and their sweetness helps balance the richness of the broth. And if that isn't enough, I have snuck in some herbed spaetzle. These dumplings are so much fun to make, and they are incredibly versatile. They're delicious in this soup, and even better on their own with just some butter and Parmesan (isn't everything?).

The technique for the spaetzle is so simple it will make you laugh. However, the broth is a two-day affair. Please don't rush—the beauty of the soup is that all the components can be made ahead, and the length of time in the fridge allows the flavors to gel and makes this better a few days later.

2 pounds (910 g) oxtail bones
with meat attached
Sea salt and freshly ground
black pepper
2 tablespoons (90 ml) olive oil,
divided
1 onion, peeled and diced
1 cup (140 g) washed and
diced carrots
1 quart chicken stock
1 cup (140 g) peeled and
diced celery root
1 cup (140 g) washed and
diced turnips
3 egg yolks
1 cup (125 g) all-purpose flour
4 tablespoons butter
1 tablespoon sliced fresh
savory

1   Preheat the oven to 350°F (175°C). Season the oxtail with salt and pepper. Place the oxtail and 2 cups of water in an enamel stockpot and roast for 3 hours.

2   Remove the stockpot from the oven and add 1 tablespoon olive oil, the onion, carrots, chicken stock, and enough water to cover, about 1 quart.

3   Bring to a boil, then reduce to a simmer, covered, and cook for 3 hours or until the meat is tender.

4   Remove the oxtail from the broth and, when cool enough to touch, extract the meat, discarding the bones.

5   In a stockpot, combine the remaining 1 tablespoon of oil, the celery root, and turnips and cook for 10 minutes on medium heat.

6   Add the oxtail meat and the broth. Season with salt and pepper and simmer for 1 hour.

7   Meanwhile, make the spaetzle: Bring a 3-quart (3 L) pot of salted water to a simmer.

8   Mix the egg yolks and flour together with ¾ cup water, then mix ½ teaspoon sea salt into the batter.

9   Shape the spaetzle by passing the batter through a colander; make sure to make 1-inch (2.5 cm) strands.

10 Cook the strands in the simmering water. The spaetzle will take about 3 to 5 minutes to cook; taste for doneness. When cooked, remove with a spider or slotted spoon, toss the spaetzle in the butter, and add to the soup. Garnish with the savory and serve.

CAULIFLOWER SOUP

SERVES 6

Sea salt
2 heads white or orange
   cauliflower, outer leaves
   and stem removed
6 tablespoons (85 g) butter
1 onion, diced
3 cloves garlic
1 cup (240 ml) Winter Pesto
   (page 251)

Here is a delicious winter warmer. Cauliflower is a particularly hardy vegetable that truly benefits from proper and sufficient cooking to reveal its inner soul. The way to coax out the best from cauliflower is slow and low. There are many varieties available these days: the familiar white, green, and even orange. My main tip is to use everything—the outer leaves, stalk, woody core, and flowers!

The finishing touch to this soup is the pesto. Made with garlic, parsley, pine nuts, and Parmesan, it is both fun and simple to make and will keep for a couple of weeks in the fridge.

1   Heat a pot of slightly salted simmering water, add the whole heads of cauliflower, and simmer until cooked through, 15 to 20 minutes.

2   Remove the cauliflower and reserve 3 cups (720 ml) of the cooking liquid.

3   In a stockpot, heat the butter over medium heat, add the onion and garlic, and cook slowly for 20 minutes, or until translucent.

4   Add the cauliflower and 3 to 4 cups (480 ml) of the cooking liquid.

5   Using an immersion blender or stand blender, puree the soup until almost liquid. Add the pesto and puree some more, adding more cooking liquid if needed.

6   Season with salt and serve hot.

CHICKEN SOUP

peas, carrots, radishes, yellow beans, and basil oil

SERVES 4

Sea salt
1 large (3½-pound/1.6 kg) chicken
2 onions, peeled and sliced
1 head of garlic, cut in half
2 tablespoons fresh parsley leaves
2 tablespoons fresh parsley stems
2 branches fresh thyme
2 bay leaves
1 cup (145 g) shelled peas
1 cup (110 g) topped and diced yellow beans
1 cup (140 g) peeled and diced carrots
1 cup (140 g) washed and diced radishes
¼ cup (60 ml) Basil Oil (page 251)

This is a very colorful and satisfying soup. The tip here is to make a chicken stock that is clear, rich, and flavorful without being salty. It takes time, and patience.

The combined vegetables are true eye candy and they are extremely healthy and pure. This is a soup that can morph with the seasons; you can add winter vegetables like parsnips and leeks or summer vegetables like zucchini and baby tomatoes. The basil oil contributes a delicious, spicy and fresh note, as well as lending a gorgeous green tint to the clear broth.

1   In a stockpot combine 4 quarts (3.8L) cold water and a pinch of salt.

2   Bring to a boil and add the chicken, onions, garlic, parsley, thyme, and bay leaves.

3   Bring to a full boil, and then reduce the heat to the lowest it will go. Cook the stock for 2 hours.

4   Remove the chicken, let cool, then remove the skin and slice the breast meat into slivers and set the meat aside. (Save the thigh and drumstick meat for another use, such as tacos.)

5   Continue cooking the stock for 3 hours more. Strain through a fine-mesh sieve lined with paper towels or cheese cloth.

6   Pour the broth into a clean pot and bring to a simmer.

7   Add the peas, beans, carrots, and radishes to the broth, along with the slivered chicken breast. Cook for 5 minutes or until the vegetables are just tender.

8   Add the basil oil and serve hot.

SOLE CRUDO

blood orange, pistachios, and Fresno chile

SERVES 4

8 ounces (225 g) very fresh
    fillet of sole or fluke
2 blood oranges
1 shallot, minced
1 Fresno chile, seeded and
    minced
4 tablespoons (60 ml) avocado
    oil
2 tablespoons shelled
    pistachios, toasted in a
    325°F (165°C) oven for 8
    minutes
1 tablespoon chopped chives

Grey sole is a special fish. Practically no one except fishermen and Chinese restaurateurs seems to use it. It is a particularly fine fish, with the same flavor and texture profile as Dover sole! The grey sole's flesh is delicate and flaky, has a low degree of fat, and is super tasty. It is terrific for sushi and, in this guise, marries with the blood orange, toasted pistachios, and oil. The final note of the mild, flavorful Fresno chiles rounds out the dish.

1   Chill a large (a 12-inch/30 cm) oval or round serving plate.

2   Trim the fish of any bones. Cut into 12 to 16 pieces and keep in the refrigerator.

3   Zest 1 blood orange, then cut both oranges into sections and save all the juice.

4   Combine the shallot, chile, and blood orange zest and juice and whisk in the oil.

5   Place the pieces of sole evenly over the cold plate, arrange the blood orange sections over them, sprinkle with the pistachios and chives, and top with the shallot–blood orange sauce. Serve immediately.

CHICKEN LIVERS

pear mostarda, upland cress, and croutons

SERVES 4

Back in 1979, I was the chef at Michael's in Santa Monica. It was a pivotal restaurant and a pivotal time for me as a cook. I was nibbling at the heels of France's young Turk chefs like Roger Vergé, Jean and Pierre Troisgros, and Michel Guérard, all truly outstanding chefs. These chefs were rapidly transforming the landscape in France and beyond with revolutionary food.

I was buoyed up by the enthusiasm at Michael's from my fellow cooks: Roy Yamaguchi, Mark Peel, Nancy Silverton, and others. These intrepid chefs helped me on my quest. I tried my hand at many traditional foods and recipes. I wanted to emulate the style and inventiveness of those French guys. One of the dishes that I tackled was a traditional chicken liver terrine. I aimed high and started experimenting with different styles.

One of the ideas was to use seasonal sourced apples or pears to help with the sweetness and acidity. Another idea was to use cooked onions and garlic. This recipe will call for both and some booze! The booze will brighten up the recipe and give some perkiness to the mousse. The pears and onions will counterbalance each other and lend a myriad of flavors. The butter will add some needed fat and texture.

It is sad that in America we tend to discard the livers that we get when we purchase a whole bird at the grocery store. If you have the means, collect them in your freezer until you have enough for this recipe (about six chickens' worth). It will amaze you what you will make from an ingredient that is essentially free. *recipe continues*

8 ounces (225 g) chicken livers, cleaned
Sea salt
6 tablespoons (90 ml) avocado oil
4 tablespoons butter
1 small onion, diced
2 cloves garlic, smashed
1 shallot, minced
3 tablespoons grappa or brandy
6 tablespoons (90 ml) heavy cream
1 baguette
Olive oil
1 cup (180 g) sliced pears
1 tablespoon mustard seeds
½ teaspoon ground turmeric
1 cup (25 g) upland cress, washed and cut into equal lengths

1   Dry the livers and season them with salt. In a cast-iron skillet, heat the avocado oil to smoking and then carefully add the livers.

2   Sauté on all sides, about 4 minutes per side, remove from the pan, and set aside to cool.

3   To the skillet, add 2 tablespoons of the butter and the onion, garlic, and shallot. Cook until tender.

4   Deglaze the pan with 1 tablespoon of the grappa. Season with salt, add half of the cream, and let cool.

5   In a food processor, combine the chicken livers and onion-cream mixture, pulse them three or four times until almost smooth, then add the remaining 1 tablespoon butter and 3 tablespoons cream and pulse until homogenous. Blend in 1 tablespoon grappa and season with salt.

6   Chill the liver mousse for 3 hours.

7   Preheat the oven to 350°F (175°C). Cut the baguette crosswise into croutons, toast in the oven until golden, then brush with olive oil.

8   In a saucepan, combine ½ cup (90 g) of the pears with the remaining 1 tablespoon grappa, the mustard seeds, turmeric, and remaining 1 tablespoon butter over low heat. Cook for 5 minutes, until thickened, then let the pear mostarda cool.

9   Cover each crouton with liver mousse and garnish with pear mostarda and upland cress.

BRUSCHETTE

Let's face it; a baguette is perfect bread. Where I grew up, baguettes really did not exist, but delicious sourdough loafs did. The great Venetian bakery in San Francisco (sadly defunct) made heroic breads, and now Acme (Steve Sullivan's magical bakery) carries on the tradition. There are some fabulous baguettes in the United States: Tartine, Gjusta, Le Pain Quotidian, and others. There are some par-baked products that are pretty damned good, but the best baguettes are in France. Maybe it is the air, the water, the flour, or the ovens; whatever it is, a baguette in Paris is a very desirable commodity.

Bruschette are a huge anchor on the menu at Barbuto. We actually prefer to use a ciabatta loaf for these in the restaurant, but at home I gravitate to a baguette. Whatever bread you choose is probably going to be good as long as you practice a couple of steps. Long ago, Alice Waters taught me the value of grilling sliced bread until golden brown, then rubbing the grilled portion with a raw garlic clove. Then very lightly slather the bread with olive oil. This sets the tone for bruschette; the toppings just add variety and nuance.

Peas and Ricotta Bruschetta

**SERVES 4 AS
AN APPETIZER**

1 cup very fresh ricotta
2 tablespoons butter, softened
2 tablespoons chopped mixed
herbs (sage, parsley, thyme,
    chives, etc.)
Sea salt
4 large slices of sourdough
    bread
1 clove garlic, cut in half
1 tablespoon olive oil
1 cup cooked peas
2 tablespoon grated Parmesan
2 ounces pea shoots or
    microgreens

Simplicity at its best—I wonder sometimes that my colleagues tend to add one or two extra ingredients that can overcomplicate a tender dish. This is drop-dead simple: peas, herbs, ricotta, and a bit of butter. In this fashion, one tastes all the ingredients, both as a whole and individually. The peas should be bought when they are at their peak; if not, honestly, frozen will be better. Herbs can vary according to the season and availability. I like sage and chives; they marry well together.

1 In a bowl, mix the ricotta, butter, and herbs and season with sea salt.

2 Toast the bread in a hot oven and rub one side with the garlic. Drizzle with the olive oil on the garlic side, then smear about one-fourth of the ricotta mixture on each piece of toast. Top each bruschetta with one-fourth of the peas, gently nudging them into the ricotta mixture.

3 Garnish with a dusting of grated Parmesan and the pea shoots.

Blue Crab Bruschetta

SERVES 4

1 pint (270 g) cooked blue
    crab meat
½ cup (120 ml) Aioli (page
    249)
1 tablespoon minced fresh
    chives, plus more for
    garnish
2 teaspoons fresh lemon juice
4 large slices of sourdough
    bread
1 tablespoon (90 ml) olive oil

Here we get a bit fancy-pants with a blue crab salad. But trust me, it is soooo simple!

1   Preheat the oven to 400°F (205°C).

2   Mix the crab with the aioli, chives, and lemon juice.

3   Cut the sourdough into crostini. Bake until golden brown.

4   In a bowl, toss the crostini with the olive oil.

5   Top each crostino with 1 tablespoon of the crab salad. Garnish with chives.

Wild Mushrooms, Ricotta, and Parsley Bruschetta

SERVES 4 AS
AN APPETIZER

1 baguette
1 clove garlic, peeled and
    halved
2 tablespoons olive oil, divided
2 cups diced wild mushrooms
2 shallots, minced
2 tablespoons Madeira
2 tablespoons butter
1 tablespoon chopped
    fresh parsley, plus 2
    tablespoons whole leaves
Sea salt and freshly ground
    black pepper
½ cup (120 ml) ricotta

As you can guess, I am huge fan of wild anything! But in particular, wild mushrooms. In spring we look for morels. These Christmas-tree-shaped mushrooms are in my top three. They are earthy, musty, supple, and delicious. Then come the chanterelles or girolles. These golden-hued open-gill mushrooms are my second favorite; they have an egg-like flavor and really yield their intrinsic charms when cooked in garlic and butter. But the king of wild mushrooms, for me at least, is the porcini. These are truly magnificent beasts! They are spectacular raw, cooked, roasted, or grilled—they are truly a well-rounded athlete.

If you have access to a great market or farm stand, then do a mixture of wild mushrooms. The different textures, flavors, colors, and odors will astound you. Mushrooms remind me why I love cooking; they are a big part of the magic.

1   Split the baguette in half lengthwise. Scoop out the center of each half, forming a channel.

2   Toast the baguette in a hot oven for 8 minutes. Rub the baguette with half a clove of the raw garlic. When nicely anointed with garlic, sprinkle with 1 tablespoon of the oil.

3   In a saucepan heat the remaining 1 tablespoon oil, then add the mushrooms and shallots. Cook over fairly high heat for 5 minutes, then deglaze the pan with the Madeira.

4   Add the butter and let cool.

5   Add the chopped parsley and season with salt and pepper. Add the ricotta and mix well.

6   Fill both halves of the baguette with the ricotta mixture and then cut into bite-sized pieces.

7   Garnish with parsley leaves and serve.

Tuna Tonnato Bruschetta

4 large slices of sourdough
     bread
4 tablespoons (60 ml) olive oil
1 (6-ounce) can or jar of oil-
     packed imported tuna
½ cup (120 ml) Aioli (page
     249)
2 tablespoons Basil Oil (page
     251)
4 tablespoons Tomato Sauce
     (page 249)
Sea salt and freshly ground
     black pepper

My wife adores canned tuna. There is magic in the can! Let's cut to the chase about canned products: they can be really terrific or they can be horrible. It is really a matter of judicious shopping, trial and error. Not all canned tunas are good, and the can will not last forever (unlike some canned goods). This recipe relies heavily on cans—for the tuna and the tomatoes. My friend Chris Bianco, the world's premier pizzaiolo, makes a delicious canned tomato product from California—Bianco DiNapoli tomatoes. I suggest you try it. I am fortunate that my buddy Anthony Giglio from *Food & Wine* is married to a Sicilian whose mother makes tomato preserves. When I say they are the best, that doesn't begin to do them justice. You cannot buy this product and I got one jar last year!

Open a can of tuna, gently fold in some aioli, add some tomato ragù and basil oil, then spread it on the grilled baguette, and you might faint from pleasure!

1   Preheat the oven to 400°F (205°C).

2   Bake the sourdough until golden brown, then slather the toast with olive oil.

3   Mix the tuna with the aioli, basil oil, and tomato sauce. Season with salt and pepper.

4   Top the bruschetta with the tomato-tuna mixture and serve.

Fontina and Ramp Bruschetta

1 cup (55 g) trimmed and
   sliced ramps
3 tablespoons olive oil, divided
1 Fresno chile, seeded and
   minced
2 teaspoons grated fresh
   ginger
Sea salt and freshly ground
   black pepper
4 large slices of sourdough
   bread
1 clove garlic, peeled and
   halved
4 ounces (105 g) fontina
   cheese, grated
1 tablespoon chopped chives

Ramps are this essence of spring. Throughout the very cold and dreary winter months in New York we dream of strawberries, asparagus, and the arrival of spring. The winter can drag on forever, but when you least expect it, up come the daffodils, the harbinger of things to come. Ramps come in at a mere trickle, then a bit more, followed by a literal assault of ramps. This member of the lily family is ubiquitous as the snow melts. We use ramps in cocktails with gin, and in pastas as a substitute for garlic or onions.

Ramps are particularly good in egg tarts, with steaks, and as a foil to other spring vegetables. They are easy to use and make great sauces to keep. Here we use them like a *conserva*, or compote. The ramps are gently cooked in olive oil with Fresno chiles and fresh grated ginger, then cooled and flavored with fontina and chives. This *conserva* is used on grilled ciabatta and in turn is garnished with fontina that we melt in the broiler. A superb appetizer.

1   In a saucepan, cook the ramps in 2 tablespoons of oil with the chile and ginger, very slowly over low heat for 15 minutes. Season with salt and pepper. Let cool.

2   Toast the sourdough in a hot oven. While the toast is hot, rub with raw garlic and then slather with the remaining 1 tablespoon oil.

3   Mix the ramps with the grated fontina.

4   Heat the broiler and top each toast with equal amounts of the ramp-fontina mixture.

5   Broil until golden, then serve hot.

6   Garnish with the chives.

CRESPELLE WITH CHESTNUT HONEY

SERVES 4

I am not a huge fan of brunch. Just like Flash in the Justice League, I wonder what all the fuss is. I remain staunchly in the minority on this. My staff has overruled me many times on many things, most vividly on the subject of brunch. Just as Flash ponders why people line up for brunch, the lines at Barbuto on Saturday and Sunday mornings are an enigma to me. Have these people been fasting all week? Whatever the reasons, weekend brunch at Barbuto is an amazing operation. Just two guys on the kitchen line toil over serving 250 folks in two hours; it's like the American Ballet Theatre on steroids.

One of the biggest hits is the crespelle. Originally (because I wanted a *lunch*, not brunch) I concocted a wilted spinach, fontina, béchamel crêpe with prosciutto and cherry tomatoes. Not bad, eh? Well, this was completely pushed aside and lost the race to a really terrific ricotta, chestnut honey crêpe that is a huge bestseller. Many years ago, at La Varenne in Paris, I was taught by the ageless Ferdinand Chambrette. He was not afraid of cream, butter, or eggs and he tutored us on the merits of using a slightly browned melted butter as an additive to the crêpe mixture. This does two things: it softens the batter and it allows for the cooking vessel to be devoid of any cooking fat. This makes for a really toothsome crêpe that is light and crispy and holds up well to any filling.

FOR THE CRÊPES:

2 eggs
½ cup (125 g) all-purpose
  flour
½ cup (240 ml) heavy cream
1 teaspoon baking powder
½ teaspoon sea salt
4 tablespoons (60 ml) melted
  butter (to really do this
  right, melt the butter in
  a hot skillet until lightly
  browned)

FOR THE FILLING:
2 tablespoons chestnut honey
½ cup (125 g) ricotta
1 teaspoon lemon zest
1 teaspoon orange zest

1   Make the crêpe batter: In a medium-sized bowl, whisk together the eggs, flour, cream, baking powder, salt, and melted butter until smooth.

2   Heat a 6-inch (15 cm) cast-iron pan over medium heat. Ladle in 3 to 4 tablespoons batter, tilt the pan to coat the bottom of the pan with the batter, and cook for 30 to 45 seconds, until the edges begin to brown, then flip and cook the other side for 5 to 10 seconds. Remove to a plate. Repeat with the remaining batter to make 12 crêpes in all; keep them covered with a clean kitchen towel.

3   Make the filling: In a small bowl, whisk together the ricotta, 1 tablespoon of the honey, the lemon zest, and orange zest.

4   In the hot skillet, reheat the crêpes one at a time and fill each one with the filling, fold in half, and serve. Drizzle the remaining 1 tablespoon honey over the crêpes just before serving.

ASPARAGUS AND PROSCIUTTO

SERVES 4

Sea salt
16 jumbo asparagus spears
8 slices prosciutto
1 tablespoon grated pecorino
    cheese

Let's face it: Asparagus is a godlike vegetable, truly a special item. The canned or jarred variety just doesn't do it for me. I grew up with Central Valley asparagus. Not realizing my great fortune, I thought all asparagus were bright green, stalky, grassy, and delicious. If you do not live near a farm, store-bought can be disappointing. Also, in years past, hothouse or foreign-grown were widely available. To this day we find Peruvian, Mexican, German, and other import asparagus in our markets. Not exactly the best carbon footprint, but boy those white asparagus are terrific when fresh. My dad made pilgrimages to Germany to eat quark spaetzle (spaetzle enfused with farmer's cheese—yum!) and morels with white asparagus.

I am a little more pedestrian in my tastes—I like fresh asparagus, steamed, grilled, or griddled (not too long), cooled, and wrapped with a good slice of prosciutto. Simplistic as all hell but wonderful! This is a go-to recipe for receptions at Barbuto; people love it!

1   In a large pot of boiling, salted water, cook the asparagus until al dente, about 8 minutes, plunge the stalks into a bowl of cold water, and then pat dry.

2   Cut the prosciutto slices in half and wrap one slice around the tip of each asparagus stalk.

3   Roll each tip in the pecorino and serve with cocktails.

ZUCCHINI CAVIAR

SERVES 4

4 very fresh zucchini (smallish in size, 4–6 inches/ 10–15 cm long)
Sea salt
4 tablespoons olive oil, divided
1 small baguette
2 shallots, minced
2 cloves garlic, 1 thinly sliced and 1 cut in half
2 teaspoons capers
¼ cup (40 g) diced green olives
2 tablespoons minced fresh basil
2 tablespons grated Parmesan

A nice way to start a meal. Best, truly, in the middle of summer. I recommend using smallish zucchini that are very fresh, and you should use as many colors as you can find. The trick here is to grill the sliced zucchini. Once they have cooled, then you get to show off your knife skills to dice the cooked slices into the most uniform size possible. The rest of the dish is a slam dunk.

1   Slice the zucchini lengthwise, ½ inch (1.25 cm) thick. Season with sea salt and toss with 1 tablespoon of the olive oil. In a cast-iron skillet over medium-high heat, sear the zucchini on both sides. Remove and let cool, then very finely dice.

2   In a pan, heat 1 tablespoon oil over medium heat, add the shallots, sliced garlic, capers, and olives and sauté briefly. Remove from the heat and let cool.

3   Preheat an oven to 350°F (175°C). Slice the baguette lengthwise. Bake until golden, about 6 minutes, and let cool.

4   Rub the cut sides of the baguette with the halved garlic, then slather with 1 tablespoon olive oil per baguette half.

5   In a bowl, combine the zucchini and the shallot-garlic-capers-olives mixture. Add the basil and then the Parmesan and mix well. Smear the mixture over the two baguette halves.

BEEF CARPACCIO AND TRUFFLES

SERVES 4

The beef industry has been trying for years to introduce veal into the mainstream of America. Somehow the thought of consuming young cows is not in our collective lexicon. I think there are many cultural issues, but I believe the color of the meat has something to do with it. Also, it is perceived as a rich person's meal, and that doesn't sit well with some folks. So, during the 2008 financial crisis, when everyone was panicking, the beef council started to examine selling one-year to two-year steers as "young" or "yearling" beef. I don't think their hearts were in it, but they knew that Australians loved the idea. It is more sustainable, poses a smaller footprint, and there is a health benefit in eating the most sustainable meat.

The taste is remarkably similar to aged beef. The difference of a year is not that much. What you find with a younger cow is more digestibility, fewer fat lines, and a delicious iron quality that is hard to put into words.

The beef is seasoned well and then literally crisped on the outside, leaving the interior basically raw. The umami power of the pre-grilled beef is intoxicating.

12 ounces (340 g) yearling
beef tenderloin
Sea salt and freshly ground
black pepper
4 tablespoons (60 ml) olive oil
4 tablespoons butter, softened
1 ounce (28 g) black truffle,
washed and thinly sliced
1 teaspoon minced shallot
1 teaspoon grated lemon zest
1 teaspoon grated garlic
1 tablespoon minced fresh
chives
1 egg yolk
1 tablespoon grated Parmesan
cheese
4 large slices of sourdough
bread

1   Season the beef with salt and pepper. Heat a cast-iron skillet over medium heat. Add 1 tablespoon olive oil to the pan.

2   Rub the beef with 2 tablespoons of the butter, then carefully add the beef to the pan and sear on all sides. Remove and let cool.

3   Preheat the oven to 400°F (200°C).

4   Cut the beef into four equal pieces. Using a mallet and two pieces of plastic wrap, pound the beef pieces into 7- to 8-inch circles, about ⅛ inch thick.

5   Rub each of four plates with 1 teaspoon olive oil and place a circle of beef on each.

6   In a bowl, mix one-half of the truffle with the shallot, lemon zest, garlic, chives, egg yolk, 2 tablespoons olive oil, and cheese.

7   Spoon one-quarter of the mixture over each piece of beef. Sprinkle with sea salt and freshly ground pepper.

8   Rub one side of each slice of bread with the remaining 2 tablespoons butter and bake in the oven until golden brown. Remove and slice into 8 pieces.

9   Garnish the carpaccio with the remaining truffle slices and serve with the sourdough toast.

SQUASH BLOSSOMS

SERVES 4

In summertime, when we spend time in France, the kids love to help cook. The two meals most requested are pizza night (everyone makes their own) and squash blossoms. To say they are a crowd-pleaser is an understatement.

In the city of Annecy, meandering through the old city is a canal. Alongside the canal on Wednesdays, Fridays, and Sundays is the farmer's market. Some of the fruits and vegetables come from as far away as Italy, but the best are the local farm stands.

For years there was this ancient woman from a remote village up the mountainside. She had a small stand with a stool, a tiny table, and some baskets filled with what she had yanked out of the garden that morning. Her hands, wizened, dirty, and strong, would reluctantly weigh your goods and hand back the change, and she would mumble a *merci*. Her produce was without parallel. And occasionally she would bring squash blossoms.

If she was out, there was a guy just adjacent who was happy to sell a *paneau*, or wooden flat, of blossoms for 50 centimes each. That would be about three blossoms per person, since friends would join, so there were usually about twenty to twenty-five of us. The house has its own garden, and if the mountain antelopes or badgers or birds didn't get there first, there would be squash blossoms, and the kids love to pick them.

1 small zucchini, minced
1 tomato, diced
1 tablespoon minced onion
2 tablespoons fresh julienned
    basil
1 tablespoon ricotta
2 tablespoons grated
    Parmesan cheese
12 squash blossoms
1 cup (240 ml) corn oil, for
    frying
½ cup (120 ml) heavy cream
½ cup (60 g) all-purpose flour
¼ teaspoon sea salt
2 to 4 tablespoons sparkling
    water

The best time to pick is in the morning, when the ground is cool and the blossoms are just waking up. I like to refrigerate them to persevere that environment. They need a little coaxing to open up. A trick is to softly blow on them, and the flower will open up. I also don't like a ton of stuffing, a teaspoon is sufficient. The blossoms are delicate, and their flavors should stand out. The method to cook them is simple and the only advice is to ensure your oil is at 300°F (150°C); any hotter and they will burn, lower and they won't cook properly.

1   Make the filling for the blossoms: In a bowl, mix the zucchini, tomato, onion, basil, ricotta, and Parmesan.

2   Fill each of the blossoms with 1 teaspoon filling. Twist the tops to seal the flowers.

3   In a high-sided saucepan, add the oil and heat until it reaches 300°F (150°C) on a deep-fry thermometer.

4   Pour the cream into a bowl, then mix in the all-purpose flour and sea salt.

5   Add the sparkling water to create a slightly thickened batter.

6   Dip the flowers in the milk-flour mixture to lightly coat.

7   Working in batches if necessary, fry the stuffed blossoms in the oil until crisp and golden on all sides, about 4 to 5 minutes. Serve immediately.

PLANCHA SHRIMP

16 (21 to 25 count) shrimp
    (or 1½ pounds/680 g),
    peeled and butterflied
Sea salt
4 tablespoons (60 ml) olive oil,
    divided
5 medium-hot red chiles (such
    as cayenne peppers)
1 cup sliced purple spring
    onions or scallions
2 lemons, cut in half
Freshly ground black pepper

What the hell is a *plancha*, anyway? This Spanish term has taken its place in the culinary lexicon. What could that possibly mean? Well in Spain, it is a specific piece of equipment that resembles our cast-iron griddles and is placed over an open or charcoal fire. This gets incredibly hot, and it is a great way to cook, but there is a learning curve.

The standard griddle you find on an American range can work well. At my house we use a cheap square Lodge griddle that is flat on one side and has grooves on the other. It is a perfect piece of cookware. It is a bit unwieldy at cleanup time, but it is brilliant for quesadillas, grilled cheese sandwiches, pancakes, practically anything. Since it conducts heat well, it is a universal tool. For this dish I would use a griddle or a cast-iron skillet. The advantage to the skillet is control and ease of cleanup.

1   Season the shrimp with salt.

2   Heat a cast-iron skillet over medium-high heat.

3   Add 3 tablespoons of the oil, wait until the oil is smoking, then add the shrimp and the lemon halves, cut side down. Season with sea salt and pepper.

4   When the shrimp are seared on one side, turn them over and add the chiles and scallions.

5   Continue to cook until the shrimp are seared on both sides and cooked through.

6   Squeeze the juice of one half of a roasted lemon over the shrimp and drizzle with the remaining 1 tablespoon olive oil. Serve hot or at room temperature.

MEATBALLS AND POLENTA

SERVES 6 TO 8

The king of meatballs is my colleague and good friend Joey Campanaro. Joey hails from Philadelphia. South Philly to be exact. Italians from that neighborhood tend to be close-knit, die-hard Eagles fans and they love their grandma's cooking. Joey adapted his meatballs from watching his grandma at the stove. He is a very astute cook who took his heritage to a new level by adding a pecorino bun. I like that idea, but I added my favorite foil, polenta. In this case, the polenta is cooked as slowly as possible, so slow that you might wonder when in the blazes will it be done, if ever. The slow, quiet procedure is an act of love—you can't leave the stove! The meatballs can be prepared simultaneously, or do as I do and make them ahead and store them in the refrigerator.

Once the polenta is cooked, you can hold it on the stove, warm. Or if you want to prepare everything ahead, then spread the polenta onto buttered cookie sheets and chill. Then roast in the oven when you're ready; the polenta will be delicious either way.

4 tablespoons olive oil, divided

2 onions, peeled and minced

4 cloves garlic, peeled and
    smashed

Sea salt and freshly ground
    black pepper

¼ teaspoon red pepper flakes

1½ pounds ground meat
    (equal parts veal, beef,
    and pork)

½ cup (85 g) minced
    prosciutto

1 cup (50 g) breadcrumbs

2 eggs

1 cup grated Gruyère

4 tablespoons (60 ml) heavy
    cream

4 tablespoons (55 g) butter

1 (16-ounce) can San
    Marzano tomatoes

1 bunch fresh basil, separate
    stems from leaves

1½ cups heirloom ground
    corn for polenta (the
    South Carolina brands are
    nutty and delicious)

4 tablespoons (25 g) grated
    Parmesan cheese

1   In a large saucepan, heat 2 tablespoons olive oil over medium heat. Cook the onions and garlic until translucent, about 10 minutes. Season with salt and let cool.

2   In a large bowl, mix together the ground meats with the black pepper, red pepper, and sea salt.

3   Mix the onions and garlic into the meat mixture, along with the prosciutto, and then add the breadcrumbs, eggs, Gruyère, and 2 tablespoons of the cream. Chill for 1 hour.

4   Roll the meat mixture into 1½-inch (about 4 cm) round balls.

5   In a large saucepan, heat 2 tablespoons olive oil and 1 tablespoon butter over medium heat until frothy. Sauté the balls until golden on all sides, about 5 to 8 minutes, then add the tomatoes and their juices and the basil stems.

6   Reduce the heat to low and cook for 20 minutes until meatballs are cooked through. Keep warm.

7   While the meatballs and sauce cook, make the polenta. In a saucepan, heat 3 cups of cold water with a pinch of salt until simmering.

8   Slowly pour the cornmeal into the water, stirring with a wooden spoon.

9   Lower heat and cook gently for 1 hour, stirring well. Add more water if the polenta looks dry.

10   When the polenta is cooked, stir in the remaining 3 tablespoons butter, 2 tablespoons Parmesan, and 2 tablespoons cream, and season with salt.

11   Gently cut the basil leaves into strips and add the basil to the sauce.

12   Place the polenta on a large platter and cover with the sauce and meatballs.

13   Garnish with the remaining 2 tablespoons grated Parmesan.

ROSEMARY FOCACCIA

MAKES 2 LARGE LOAVES

1¼ cups (310 g) biga (page 31)
1½ cups plus 2 tablespoons
  (390 ml) warm water
6 cups (740 g) bread flour
1 teaspoon active dry yeast
1½ tablespoons kosher salt
2 tablespoons (30 ml) olive oil
Coarse sea salt
¼ cup fresh rosemary leaves

Heather Miller is my spirit baker/pastry chef. Self-taught, incredibly humble, she has a fire in her belly and makes the best baked goods in the land. Here is a prime example, her focaccia. Nowadays we all know what focaccia is: a salted, yeasty bread resembling over-risen pizza.

The best part of this bread is how easy it is to bake at home. The real tricks are simple: good oil, sea salt, a bread starter (biga), and some decent rosemary. I particularly like the bread with rosemary blossoms; these are readily available in California but may be harder to find elsewhere. Heather's methodology is quite straightforward and can even be made in a decent-sized toaster oven.

1   In the bowl of a stand mixer, combine the biga, 1¼ cup water, bread flour, and yeast. Using the dough hook, mix on low speed until the ingredients come together, then increase speed to medium high and mix for 4 to 5 minutes. Cover the dough with plastic wrap and let it rest for ½ hour.

2   Add the salt, remaining water, and olive oil and mix on low speed again until these ingredients are incorporated. Increase to medium high and mix another 3 minutes.

3   Form the dough into a ball and place in an oiled mixing bowl. Cover with plastic wrap or a kitchen towel and let rise for 1 to 2 hours, until about doubled in size.

4   Preheat the oven to 425°F (220°C). Generously oil two large cookie sheets with olive oil. Divide the dough in two, form each half into a rough ball, and lay one on each sheet pan. Rub the tops with more olive oil, cover with plastic, and set aside for about 45 minutes, until the dough feels relaxed and a little puffy.

5   Using your fingers as if you were playing piano, make indentations in the dough, pushing it out toward the sides of the pans. Sprinkle the tops evenly with the rosemary and sea salt and press them into the dough. (Don't be afraid to use plenty of rosemary and salt!)

6   Bake for 30 minutes or until golden brown. Remove and place on a cooling rack. Drizzle any extra olive oil from the baking pans over the focaccia and let cool.

PORCINI AND GARLIC

16 ounces (455 g) fresh
    porcini
2 cloves garlic, in their skins
Sea salt
Olive oil cooking spray
¼ teaspoon espelette pepper
1½ teaspoons olive oil
2 tablespoons butter
1 tablespoon minced fresh
    parsley

Cepes or porcini, the name is different the world over. They have a meaty, umami flavor that is scrumptious. Every once in a while, I receive gifts from foragers. These can come from as far as Poland or as close as New York State. The flavors can truly vary, as do their size, freshness, and variety (mycologists list more than fifty types that are edible).

On one occasion, my buddy Ruth Reichl was dining at Barbuto. I happened to have some gifted porcini. I cut them in half lengthwise, oiled them slightly, seasoned them with sea salt, and grilled them over a medium fire. On the side I slowly sweated some garlic and butter, and at the last second added some chopped Italian parsley. The mushrooms went to platter and then the garlic butter and that was it. I hope Ruth was happy.

1   Really clean the mushrooms well. Carefully cut lengthwise into ⅜-inch-thick (1 cm) slices.

2   Put the garlic cloves in a saucepan with 1 inch (2.5 cm) water and a pinch of salt. Bring to a simmer and cover. Cook for 15 minutes. Let cool and then peel and mince the garlic.

3   Using a spray olive oil, gently coat the mushrooms and then season with salt and the espelette pepper.

4   Heat a cast-iron griddle or plancha (see page 81) over medium heat and then add the mushrooms and cook until golden all over. Place in a bowl.

5   In a saucepan, heat the olive oil, butter, and minced garlic. Add the parsley and then toss the parsley and garlic butter with the mushrooms, season with salt, and serve hot.

SOCCA!

SERVES 4 (ABOUT 12 PANCAKES)

1 cup (180 g) finely ground chickpea flour
¼ cup plus 3 tablespoons (60 ml) olive oil
1 teaspoon sea salt
½ cup (120 ml) ricotta

Many years ago, I embarked on a tour of Nice. I missed the Cours Saleya, where the market takes place in the old town, shame on me! Later on, my buddy Colman Andrews, an intrepid culinarian, admonished me and took me on a personal tour. The first stop was the socca lady. Imagine an oil drum upright with holes poked in the sides. The lady had a nice fire from scraps of wood and the *Nice Matin* (local paper). She had a small umbrella and a table. She would ladle the chickpea batter on top of the drum. Now, you can picture her: a Niçoise woman from the Cours Saleya, with amazing features, makeup, high heels, and a Provençal outfit. And a cigarette perched on her lips! After ladling out the batter, she quickly flipped over the crêpe and with a twist of the wrist shoved the hot, slightly charred socca on a sheet of the *Matin* into my hand. No sauce, no filling, just a touch of sea salt. It was heaven.

1   Put the chickpea flour in a bowl and slowly whisk in 1½ cups (355 ml) cold water. Add more water if the dough is too thick (it should resemble crêpe batter).

2   Whisk in ¼ cup (60 ml) of the olive oil and the salt.

3   Heat an 8-inch nonstick pan over medium heat.

4   For each crepe, pour about ¼ cup of the batter into the middle of the pan and quickly tilt and swirl to spread the batter in a thin, even layer. Cook until almost burnt, about 1 minute, drizzle with ¼ tablespoon olive oil, and flip over carefully using a small rubber spatula to ease the crêpe from the pan if necessary. Cook on the other side for another 30 seconds until almost burnt as well. Add 2 teaspoons cheese to the center, fold up the crêpe, and eat hot!

BREADSTICKS

parmesan and balsamic vinegar

SERVES 4 TO 6

These *grissini* are a major element on the hors d'oeuvres menu at Barbuto. They are skinny, well cooked, and very crunchy. It is said the recipe was invented in Torino, the capital of Piedmont.

This recipe was originally from my partner Fabrizio Ferri, the amazing fashion photographer, educator, fashion icon, and autodidact, who grew up in Rome.

In the early days of Barbuto, we catered some crazy events for Fabrizio, usually in one of the adjacent or upstairs studios. One of these was an official launch for Alicia Keys, across the street at Fabrizio's Twelfth Street studio. Fabrizio requested a giant wheel of Parmesan. Barbuto's breadsticks had already become somewhat legendary, so I thought, let's serve them and carve out big slivers of the gorgeous product of Emilia-Romagna with breadsticks and call it a day. Fabrizio said, "Well enough, but can you add some balsamic as well?" I truly can't abide the overuse of balsamic in our foodie world. It has become synonymous with bad cooking. But I had a source of true, aged Modena Balsamic, and he was right—it was heaven!

The crowning glory of the night was the magnificent Alicia, barely out of her teens, performing solo. And to top it off, Prince was lifted over the crowd by his bodyguards so he could stand in front of the stage to pay respects. Insane! So why not try my breadsticks and throw yourself a wild party?

recipe continues

8 ounces (225 g) Pizza Dough
(page 30)
1 teaspoon sea salt
1 tablespoon olive oil, plus
more for the cookie sheet
1 wedge (1 pound/450 g) of
Parmesan
6 tablespoons (90 ml) 25-year-
aged Balsamico

1   Preheat the oven to 350°F (175°C).

2   Roll out the dough and, using a pasta cutter on the fettucine setting, cut into 12-inch (30.5 cm) strips. Place the strips on an oiled cookie sheet. Sprinkle with salt and bake for 5 minutes or until the strips just begin to color. Remove to a wire rack and let cool. Increase the oven temperature to 375°F (190°C).

3   Put the breadsticks back on the cookie sheet and bake again for 3 to 5 minutes, or until gold in color.

4   Remove and sprinkle the warm sticks with the olive oil. Let cool.

5   Serve with the cheese and vinegar.

FONDUTA

SERVES 4

4 egg yolks
¾ cup grated fontina or
    Gruyère
¾ cup (180 ml) heavy cream
½ teaspoon sea salt
3 tablespoons butter
1 baguette, cut into cubes

The pride of Piedmont. This very luxurious and decadent appetizer is a winter favorite in the cold, lovely area just south and east of the Alps. A glass of Arneis or Dolcetto makes the world go round. The Piemontese use terrific *grissini* to dip or crusty day-old levain loaves to make crostini. This dish is quite easy and fun. You need a good casserole and to plan ahead so that you can enjoy this with your guests. Please forget the cholesterol dangers here; just walk a mile before dinner and one after, and that should help mitigate any issues! The recipe closely resembles a fondue. The big difference is the egg yolks, rendering the Fonduta a bit more fragile. But it's essentially the same, a luxurious concoction of cheese, egg yolks, and more cheese!

1   Preheat the oven to 350°F (175°C).

2   In a bowl, mix the egg yolks with the cheese, cream, and salt.

3   Put the butter in a double boiler; heat over low until melted.

4   Add the egg yolk–cheese mixture and, using a wooden spoon, beat well and continuously until slightly thickened, for 10 to 15 minutes or until a thermometer reads about 170°F (76°C). If the fonduta gets too hot, move the double boiler off the heat briefly. Lower the heat to barely a murmur; keep hot.

5   In the oven, toast the bread until golden on all sides.

6   To serve, provide fondue forks to dip the bread cubes into the fonduta.

SALADS

EVERYONE WHO VISITS BARBUTO eats their salad. I am most happy about this! New York is such a fantastic source of all things salad-like, it makes it wonderfully easy to serve great stuff. In recent years, the greens available at the farmers market have tripled. In years past endive, trevisano, gem lettuces, and so on were imported. Now the local farmers have really upped their game. And we are the happy beneficiaries. The number of varieties is astounding. But a salad is not all lettuce.

I think the salad course is really the happiest part of the meal for me. I know that if the greens are delicious, the olive oil good, then the world spins a little more evenly.

In your local farmers markets, you will find wonderful seasonal ingredients for salads, such as brilliant persimmons in late fall, heirloom tomatoes in July, and English peas in June. Local asparagus is fleeting and quixotic; they can pop up from February to perhaps late June. I adore mixing the wild (chanterelle or morel mushrooms and ramps) with the sea (shrimp and lobster) with the land (lamb and pork). I do like to use the ubiquitous chicken in salads, since they are available year-round.

Lately I have embraced some fruit in salads, but no more than will make me crazy. In these recipes you will find the bitter and the sweet (grapefruit and radicchio), the hot (grilled calamari) and the cool (tomatoes and ricotta). I think you will love making these salads. They're some of my favorites.

Ingredients that augment and benefit salad compositions include interesting mustards, preserved fish, like sardines and anchovies, great garlic and shallots, citrus of all varieties, and vegetables galore. Artichokes, fennel, green onion, spring onion, avocado, tomatoes of all sizes, radishes, asparagus, zucchini. Then are the proteins: lobster, shrimp, crab and other crustaceans, chicken in all guises, squab, quail, duck, and pheasant. Then come all the meats: cured, freshly grilled, roasted, smoked, and raw. Of note are the exotica: truffles, caviar, bottarga, and the like. And we must not forget cheese and yogurt.

Barbuto follows an international bent; we appreciate Italian ingredients and recipes foremost, but flavors can range across the world. The only locales that are relatively off limits for our menu are Asian and Indian (though I do borrow their sensibilities, spices, occasional ingredients, and techniques).

The one salad that we never take off the Barbuto menu is the kale. My warm calamari is a perennial favorite as well. We aim for seasonal, and that can encompass the holidays and special occasions.

At home you have the flexibility to try a different salad every night. I suggest trying many different recipes, getting out of your comfort zone. Salads are the most forgiving of recipes, and the easiest to remedy if anything should go sideways.

KALE SALAD

anchovy vinaigrette and pecorino

SERVES 6

Let's face it, we all hated kale as kids (and some adults still do!). This is so sad, because not only will this recipe surprise and please, but it also sets the stage for an ingredient that is truly a super-food. Kale has the amazing ability to heal, to nourish, and even to extend our lives. If the color green is always a good choice with food, kale is by extension the king of green. Kale just needs some love and a little abuse to display its charms.

This recipe is simple, fast, and delicious. The "abuse" part is not crazy talk; the kale needs force in order to loosen up and reveal its flavor. There is an enzyme in kale that reacts with acid. This enzymatic reaction literally cooks the kale and renders it edible and delicious. It is a rule at Barbuto always to include a kale salad as part of one's meal, even for the folks who say they hate kale! If memory serves me, Melissa Lopez (now the chef at Bestia in Los Angeles) was my chef when the famous kale salad was devised. She should therefore lay claim to this incredible recipe. Whether she appropriated it from another source, or by her own design, "the kale" has become a Barbuto menu standby.

The salad is a simple affair, but with huge benefits and spectacular results. Many customers would be totally satisfied If we served only kale salad, JW Chicken, gnocchi, JW Potatoes, and budino. *recipe continues*

8 ounces (225 g) kale (please leave the stems intact)
6 fresh basil leaves, patted dry and rolled like a cigar
2–4 salt-cured anchovies, rinsed and deboned
2 cloves garlic, peeled, green shoots removed, and smashed
1 egg yolk, at room temperature
1 tablespoon Dijon mustard
Sea salt
1½ teaspoons red wine vinegar
1½ teaspoons fresh lemon juice
½ cup extra-virgin olive oil
Freshly ground black pepper
⅓ cup (30 g) grated Pecorino Romano cheese
1 tablespoon toasted breadcrumbs

1   Wash the kale well and dry in a salad spinner. On a wooden (this is truly important advice—plastic is impossible) cutting board, julienne the kale as thinly as possible. Place the kale in a salad bowl. Keep cold. Clean the board and wipe it dry.

2   On the cutting board, finely mince the basil. Add the anchovies and garlic and continue to mince until you achieve a paste.

3   In another bowl, combine the basil and garlic paste with the egg yolk, mustard, ½ teaspoon sea salt, red wine vinegar, and the lemon juice. Use a whisk and mix well. Drizzle in the oil, whisking continuously, until you achieve a broken emulsion.

4   Pour half of the dressing over the kale, enough to coat the leaves well, and, using as much force as possible, crush the kale and dressing. (We use our hands at Barbuto, but with gloves of course! Buy a box of surgical gloves and you will find them indispensable.) This will release the enzymes from the kale to interact with the dressing's acid and salt. This creates magic! Add a pinch of salt and a few turns of pepper.

5   Sprinkle with the cheese and breadcrumbs; toss well, taste for seasoning, and serve within 1 hour. Letting it sit for a little while does wonders for the flavor.

BABY GEM SALAD

green goddess dressing

4 small heads of gem lettuce
1 avocado, diced
1 clove garlic, smashed
1 shallot, minced
1 tablespoon fresh lemon juice
1 tablespoon sherry vinegar
1 tablespoon Dijon mustard
⅓ cup (75 ml) olive oil
2 tablespoons walnut halves

Gem lettuce is the current rage, and rightfully so. It emulates the romaine parent but has a unique "lettucy" quality. We use gem in many guises, as a scoop for hors d'ouevres with roasted duck legs, as a backdrop for grilled whole fish, or as a standalone, as in this recipe.

I love toasted walnuts. Almonds and other nuts sometimes overshadow them, but walnuts are a great food nut: They make wonderful sauces, they go well in meat dishes, and chocolate chip cookies would pale without them.

1   Cut the lettuces in half, rinse in ice-cold water, and dry.

2   Make the dressing: Put the avocado, garlic, shallot, lemon juice, vinegar, and mustard in a blender, pulse twice, then dribble in the oil while the motor is running. The dressing should be quite thick, but if it looks too thick, add a few tablespoons of cold water.

3   Crush the walnuts with the flat side of a knife.

4   In a bowl, toss the lettuce with the dressing. Scatter the salad over a large platter, then top with the walnuts and serve.

BRUSSELS SPROUTS SALAD

SERVES 4

8 ounces (225 g) Brussels sprouts
¼ cup (25 g) grated Pecorino Romano cheese
4 tablespoons (60 ml) fresh lemon juice (from about 2 lemons)
4 tablespoons (30 g) slivered almonds, toasted in a 350°F (175°C) oven for 6 to 8 minutes
Sea salt and freshly ground black pepper

This has been on the menu numerous times over the years. It has all the bells and whistles that make it a Barbuto dish: seasonal, Italian-like, using ingredients that are not in the mainstream (or at least they weren't fifteen years ago) and technique that is fun. The trick here is a sharp knife. Knives are the mainstay of any kitchen, but getting them sharp and keeping them sharp is another story. I think most folks have simply gotten used to using dull knives.

Here is some good advice: buy a Brod and Taylor knife sharpening tool. It is neat, portable, and good-looking, and it works! I keep mine in front of me in the kitchen. For those at home who are meticulous, sharpen your knives after you wash them and you will always start off with a sharp knife. Also, if you think your knife is not sharp, use a Japanese mandolin for this recipe; it is an amazing tool. Be careful not to cut yourself, however; I have many times! The shaving of the Brussels is time-consuming and actually relaxing. Just when you think you will never get through the two pints, you will be finished! The lemon collides with the enzymes in the sliced sprouts and this will create that special umami flavor that people crave.

1   Slice the Brussels sprouts very thinly on a mandolin or with a very sharp knife.

2   In a bowl, toss the Brussels sprouts with the rest of the ingredients until evenly distributed. Season well with salt and pepper. Place on a platter and serve.

MELON AND PROSCIUTTO SALAD

2 Cavaillon-style melons
 (Crenshaw are nice)
2 cups (100 g) picked purslane
 or watercress
Sea salt
4 tablespoons (60 ml) olive oil
12 slices prosciutto
1 tablespoon fresh lemon juice

Melon and prosciutto is an inevitable pairing, a perfect marriage, like shrimp and avocado or burrata and tomato. Purslane is truly an old-fashioned green. One can imagine dining on purslane at King Arthur's court or a formal dinner at Buckingham Palace. Full of flavor and nutrients, it is an interesting green. I love the smaller variety; if too big, they can be tough and inedible. This salad is simple to make and can be prepared well in advance.

1   Cut the melons in half and scoop out the seeds. Using a vegetable peeler, remove the outer husk. With a sharp knife, cut the melon into long, thin slices.

2   On a large (12-inch/30.5 cm) platter, arrange the purslane and the slices of melon. Sprinkle with salt and the oil.

3   Deftly weave the prosciutto among the melon and purslane.

4   Sprinkle with lemon juice and serve at room temperature.

CITRUS SALAD

2 blood oranges
1 grapefruit
2 Cara Cara oranges
2 tangerines
2 tablespoons olive oil
1 head of gem lettuce
1 tablespoon chopped
    Castelvetrano olives
1 shallot, minced
1 cup (240 ml) fresh ricotta
1 tablespoon chopped fresh
    parsley

I love the wintertime, in large part because it is citrus season. Nothing better than Meyer lemons, limes, oranges, pink grapefruits, and tangerines. This salad celebrates the season and is a fresh, healthy salad that perks up the appetite. I am not going to dictate the mixture; you can decide what you like and see what's in the market. I do think grapefruit is a worthy ingredient, but taste it to ensure it is not too bitter.

Oranges are swell too, but they can be almost too sweet. I do prefer Cara Cara and blood oranges, but any variety will do. Tangerines are perfect as well. The shallot will help with some acerbic qualities as well as some crunch, and the olives help tie together all the ingredients.

1   Zest the blood oranges and juice one of them.

2   Cut all the remaining citrus into sections. Mix the citrus wedges together in a bowl, including any juice; add the blood orange zest and juice and the oil.

3   Wash and dry the lettuce. Separate the small leaves and cut up the bigger leaves if necessary. Put in a bowl and add the citrus sections, olives, and shallot and gently toss two times, then turn the salad onto a platter.

4   Garnish with dabs of the ricotta and the parsley and serve.

HEIRLOOM PANZANELLA

1 baguette-shaped loaf (250 g) of nice bread, such as sourdough, ciabatta, or traditional baguette
1 clove garlic, peeled and halved
10 tablespoons (150 ml) olive oil
4 heirloom tomatoes (about 2 pounds)
Sea salt
2 tablespoons red wine vinegar or more to taste
2 tablespoons Basil Oil (page 251)
1 tablespoon minced shallot
12 fresh basil leaves, torn

Panzanella was created as a frugal way to stretch some lovely tomatoes and make the most of day-old crusty bread. The acidic juices of the tomatoes perk up and soften the bread. And in this fashion, the salad becomes hearty and nutritious for a few pennies.

We still appreciate this frugality and celebrate the marriage of bread and tomatoes. Though at Barbuto we use great levain bread, heirloom tomatoes, and basil oil. The basil oil makes it all work; it is the flavor catalyst that gives the dish its groove. You'll need big, hearty beefsteak tomatoes that are just ripe. They should be dense, sweet, and acidic but hold together well. Good olive oil is essential. Find some hearty levain or sourdough, most supermarkets have it, or you can make your own or order it online.

1 Preheat the oven to 400°F (205°C).

2 Split the baguette in half lengthwise. Toast in the oven until golden brown. When cool, rub the cut sides of the bread with the garlic clove and then slather with 8 tablespoons of the oil.

3 Cut the baguette into half-moon slices.

4 Cut out the stems of the tomatoes, cut the tomatoes in half, and sprinkle them with salt and the remaining 2 tablespoons oil. Place in a baking pan, cut sides up, and bake the tomatoes for 10 minutes. Let cool, then roughly chop the tomatoes. Transfer to a bowl and add the baguette slices, vinegar, basil oil, and shallot. Gently toss to combine.

5 Add the basil and season with salt. The salad can sit in the refrigerator for an hour. Serve cool.

CALAMARI SALAD

1 cup very fresh squid
1 cup rock shrimp
Sea salt and cracked black
   pepper
3 tablespoons extra-virgin
   olive oil
¼ cup (30 g) sliced radishes
½ cup (120 ml) rosé wine
½ cup (120 ml) Aioli
   (page 249)
½ teaspoon minced Fresno
   chile
1 teaspoon fresh lemon juice
¼ cup (13 g) mixed chopped
   fresh herbs (such as
   parsley, chives, and
   arugula)
1 head each radicchio and
   Little Gem lettuce
1 cup (40 g) frisée lettuce

I was such a picky eater as a child. I have no patience for chefs with perfect childhood memories who can recall their first sea urchin, which they ate while perched on Daddy's knee at Club 55 in St. Tropez, while sipping watered-down rosé at the bright young age of five! At five I would not touch a clam, or a lobster, and god forbid squid! And urchins— forget about it!

And now I crave seafood. Here is a great way to celebrate the ocean and marry the bounty of the land with that of the sea. It is actually an easy dish to make, and it can be served as a main course. At Barbuto, this would be an appetizer, served with a crusty baguette and some cold white wine.

1   Toss the squid and rock shrimp in a medium bowl with salt and cracked pepper.

2   Heat a 10-inch (25 cm) cast-iron skillet over medium-high heat until very hot. Add 1 tablespoon of the oil. When smoking, tenderly add the squid, shrimp, and the radishes. Be careful, a flame may erupt. Stir with a metal spoon for about 3 minutes.

3   Add the wine and deglaze the pan. Remove from the heat then fold in the aioli, chile, and lemon juice and stir quickly; season with salt and black pepper and fold in the herbs.

4   Quickly transfer to the bowl with the lettuces and toss well to slightly wilt the greens. Correct the seasoning. Serve warm.

RED GODDESS SALAD

This is really an innovative and, at the same time, traditional dish. What does it have to do with Italy? Not much; it does have a lot to do with me. So, I guess therein lies the dichotomy: Barbuto can be playful and adventuresome, classical and forward-looking at the same time.

I love nothing better than a ripe, perfect avocado. And there was a time when the red bell peppers of California were my go-to ingredient. It makes sense to invite these two into a salad. I think the Goddess part is especially fun, since I want the peppers and the avocado to be the gods. The other ingredients are the foil and the delicacy of this dish—red oak leaf lettuces and a dressing that uses soft, smoky grilled peppers, partially accented by Meyer lemon. The herbs are basil and chives, the latter adding a perky onion note. Once the peppers have been cooked and prepared and the dressing made, the rest is very straight-forward, and the result will please you.

2 red bell peppers
Juice of 1 Meyer lemon (about
    4 tablespoons)
⅓ cup (30 g) minced scallions
    (about 3 small scallions)
1 egg yolk
Sea salt
12 fresh basil leaves (about
    ¼ ounce/8 g)
¼ cup (60 ml) plus 1 table-
    spoon avocado oil
1 head of red oak leaf lettuce
2 tablespoons minced fresh
    chives
1 ripe avocado

1 Preheat the oven to broil. Roast the peppers on a baking sheet and then put them in a covered bowl to steam. Seed them and remove the charred skin.

2 Using a food processor, puree one pepper with the Meyer lemon juice, scallions, and egg yolk. Add salt and the basil and pulse to combine.

3 With the food processor running, drizzle in ¼ cup (60 ml) of the avocado oil to form a dressing. Season with salt.

4 Wash and dry the lettuce and cut the leaves into bite-sized pieces. Put it in a large bowl.

5 Dice the remaining roasted red pepper and add it to the lettuce, along with the chives and remaining 1 tablespoon avocado oil.

6 Peel, pit, and dice the avocado and add it to the bowl.

7 Add 3 tablespoons of the dressing and gently toss the salad. Taste to ensure that there is enough dressing and add more if necessary. Taste for seasoning and serve.

CAESAR SALAD

SERVES 6

Is this an Italian salad? I say, but of course! The salad originated at the Hotel Caesar in Tijuana, a serious watering hole that served Italian food. Rumor has it that it was invented for a dignitary, perhaps a movie star. The rest of the story is murky at best. My mother was infatuated with this dish. Visiting Hotel Caesar in the early 1960s, she learned the recipe firsthand.

The Caesar of the story was an Italian immigrant from Piedmont. The story goes that his daughter was working the kitchen one night, but not much was available when the dignitary arrived. Caesar evidently came up with this concoction, which of course he named for himself!

I am fortunate to be friends with Carolynn Carreño, whose dad had worked as a waiter at the hotel and later had a restaurant across the street. In any case, I have adapted Carolynn's dad's recipe and put a couple of twists on it. One, I grill the whole heads of romaine! This is a great technique that is easy to do and lends a smoky, charred note to the salad. And instead of the fried croutons, I grill baguettes and rub them with garlic and olive oil. I also use Meyer lemon instead of lime. The last twist is the addition of basil, which gives the salad a little boost without being pretentious.

3 heads of romaine lettuce, outer leaves removed, washed, dried, and cut in half
¼ cup (60 ml) avocado oil
Sea salt
1 baguette, cut in half lengthwise
1 clove garlic, halved, plus 2 cloves smashed
2 tablespoons plus ¼ cup (60 ml) olive oil
2 egg yolks
4 anchovy fillets, two chopped roughly, and two torn for garnish
Juice of 1 Meyer lemon
4 tablespoons (25 g) grated Parmesan cheese
12 fresh basil leaves
10 grinds of black pepper

1 Heat a grill and clean the grate well. Toss the heads of romaine in the avocado oil and season with salt. Grill on all sides, turning quickly so as to not burn the lettuces. When grilled, place in a bowl and cover to let the lettuces steam.

2 Grill the baguette, then rub with the halved garlic and drizzle with the 2 tablespoons olive oil. Tear into bite-sized pieces.

3 In a bowl, using a small whisk, whisk together the egg yolks, smashed garlic, anchovies, and ¼ teaspoon salt. Whisk in the Meyer lemon juice. Add 2 tablespoons of the cheese and then drizzle in the olive oil, whisking continuously until you achieve a blended sauce. Mince the basil and add to the sauce. Season with salt and 10 grinds of pepper.

4 Separate the leaves of romaine but leave them whole, add the sauce, and toss well.

5 Place on a platter and garnish with the pieces of grilled baguette. Sprinkle with the remaining 2 tablespoons cheese and serve.

FRISÉE, RADICCHIO, AND PEAR SALAD

SERVES 4

2 pears, ripe but not too soft
½ cup (50 g or 70 g) walnuts
    or hazelnuts
1 head frisée
2 heads radicchio
2 tablespoons champagne
    vinegar
3 tablespoons olive oil
Sea salt and freshly ground
    black pepper
1 tablespoon chopped fresh
    chives

A true classic of wintertime at Barbuto. The bitter, sharp, and almost inedible nature of radicchio has charmed us. Perhaps the bitterness implies healthful; at the very least it is full of vitamins and roughage. I have always adored pears. Comice, Bosc, Anjou are all incredible, and while they can be on the sweet side, slightly underripe they marry well with radicchio. The frisée is the fun part of the dish. From the same family as radicchio (endive), it has bright-green nose-tickling leaves that are not as bitter, and perhaps more toothsome. The bright purple-red of the radicchio, the brilliant green of the frisée, and the cool crispy sweetness of the pear make for a scrumptious winter salad.

1   Preheat the oven to 300°F (150°C).

2   Stem and seed the pears.

3   Spread the nuts on a baking sheet and toast in the oven for 8 minutes.

4   Wash and separate the leaves of the frisée.

5   Wash the radicchio, pull it apart, and tear it into bite-size pieces.

6   To make the dressing, whisk together the vinegar and olive oil. Season with sea salt and pepper.

7   Slice the pears and, in a salad bowl, toss them with the lettuces and dressing.

8   Add the chives and toss again.

SHAVED VEG SALAD

carrots, asparagus, watermelon radishes, celery, and mint

SERVES 4

4 heirloom carrots, washed
 and topped, thinly sliced
 lengthwise
1 bunch thick asparagus,
 washed and thinly sliced
 lengthwise
3 watermelon radishes,
 washed and thinly sliced
 crosswise
6 stalks young celery,
 washed and thinly sliced
 lengthwise
3 tablespoons toasted
 hazelnuts, roughly
 chopped
1 tablespoon fresh lemon juice
2 tablespoons olive oil
Sea salt and freshly ground
 black pepper
A few mint leaves, for garnish

Here is a wonderful salad. It makes a gorgeous start to a meal and is the healthiest plate of food I can imagine. The colors alone make this salad vibrant, sassy, and bold. The technique is the simplest. Just buy a great vegetable peeler and get to work. Of course, you should get the finest vegetables possible. I often ponder the bigger picture of the world of food. Questions about how to feed the world in twenty-five years. What makes sense for future generations to explore as alternative food sources. I think this salad is the epitome of the future: vegetables that are hardy, tasty, and give you the biggest bang for the buck.

1   Toss all the ingredients together, seasoning with salt and pepper, garnish with mint leaves, and serve.

PRIMI ~ PASTA, RISOTTO AND GRAINS

IN ITALY there is a specific sequence to a meal. Americans are still confused by the progression; but I personally love it. Antipasti of salumi, bread, olives, marinated peppers, followed by some fried artichoke hearts, perhaps scallop tartare, or crepes with ham and béchamel. And then the primi course. This, for me, is the make-or-break course. It will decide whether a restaurant deserves its laurels or not. This course is not meant to be the main event when dining out; a fish course follows and then the main event—either meat or poultry.

The portion size of the primi course is super important. It should be tantalizing but not overdone. It is really a special event, were the chef can show off his or her skill set. If served individually, a small plate or bowl is all you need. If one serves family style, as we do at Barbuto, the idea is to try two or three different tastes: a gnocchi, some risotto, maybe a Bolognese with strozzapreti or some farro with braised celery hearts. Whatever the content, the primi should be flavorful, not overwhelming, and extremely tasty!

BUCATINI WITH PESTO

Swiss chard

SERVES 4

Sea salt
1 cup (95 g) freshly shelled
  walnuts
3 cloves garlic, smashed
½ cup fresh Italian parsley
  leaves
Freshly ground black pepper
½ cup (120 ml) olive oil
12 ounces (340 g) bucatini
¼ cup (35 g) sliced onion
1 cup (100 g) chopped chard
  stems
2 tablespoons butter
¼ cup (25 g) grated Parmesan
  cheese

Here is a great rebound. The bucatini noodle is fascinating; a fat spaghetti that has a tunnel! The pesto is a winter version: parsley, toasted walnuts, Parmesan, and reserved garlic. The chard is the rebound part. Most cooks abandon the stems in favor of the leaves, and I never have understood why. The stems are nutritious and crisp, and the best part is flavor; these guys have it in spades.

1   Preheat the oven to 300°F (150°C).

2   Prepare a pot of boiling, salted water.

3   Toast the walnuts in the oven for 8 minutes. Let cool.

4   Put the garlic, parsley, walnuts, ¼ teaspoon salt, and a few turns of black pepper in a food processor. Pulse the machine and add ¼ cup (60 ml) of the oil. Pulse until the pesto has a creamy consistency.

5   Drop the pasta into the boiling water.

6   In a large saucepan, heat the remaining ¼ cup (60 ml) oil. Add the onion, cook for 4 minutes, then add the chard stems. Cook until tender, about 4 minutes.

7   When al dente, drain the pasta, reserving ½ cup pasta water.

8   Add the pasta to the saucepan, then ½ cup (120 ml) of the pesto and the butter (reserve the rest of the pesto for another dish). Toss the chard stems, onion, pasta, butter, and pesto together; add the reserved ½ cup pasta water and the cheese.

9   Toss again and season with salt and black pepper. Serve hot.

LITTLE FISH RISOTTO

onions, parsley, saffron, and Chenin Blanc

SERVES 4

In 2018, Marriott Hotels, in conjunction with *Food & Wine* magazine, launched a Food & Wine festival in Venice, Italy. Happy to be on board, I spent almost a week at the idyllic Marriott resort in the bay just west of San Marco. The shuttle boats would leave every half hour, so getting to a favored spot was not difficult.

The editor of *Food & Wine*, Hunter Lewis, is a Barbuto "graduate." He put in his time at Barbuto and things turned out okay for him. He had heard me tell of the almost mythical Gatto Nero (black cat) restaurant located on the island of Burano to the east of Venice. So he commandeered a gorgeous Venetian water taxi and we set off for lunch. When I say mythical, here is the truth.

I scour guidebooks as a vocation. One restaurant that caught my eye years ago was the Gatto Nero. Burano is an easy trip from the Rialto Bridge, but a fair walk from San Marco. For my wife Sally's birthday in 2016 we made a reservation and embarked to Burano (we went by *vaporetto*, not a fancy taxi). Sitting in a group of ten under a large umbrella on the dock, we had one of the more memorable meals of my life.

My son Alexander, who was a graduating senior on his way to college, had been a fussy eater in his younger days. Now, almost a full-fledged adult, his palate had changed. One of the many dishes we had was a risotto. The waiter brought out a simple stainless-steel oval platter with what appeared to be rice and broth. And that's what it was. But what rice and what broth!

6 tablespoons (90 ml) olive oil
2 onions, minced
1 head of garlic, split into cloves
1 pound (455 g) fish bones (from flat fish or rock fish; ask your local fishmonger)
1 fish head (not from an oil fish or salmon)
1 cup (50 g) fresh parsley stems
2 cups (480 ml) Chenin Blanc
8 cups water
¼ teaspoon saffron
1½ cups (285 g) Arborio rice
Sea salt and freshly ground black pepper

Alexander proclaimed his first mouthful the best food he'd ever had. My first bite was the same. The waiter explained that the local fishermen would catch tiny baitfish along the shores of Burano, and then the chef would prepare a broth from these little fish. Just as in St. Tropez, where the local catch is made essentially into a seafood health serum as bouillabaisse, Gatto Nero did the same and added rice. Here is my version of the heavenly dish.

1 Prepare the fish stock: In a medium pot, heat 2 tablespoons of the oil over medium heat and add two-thirds of the onion and all of the garlic. Sweat for 10 minutes over low heat.

2 Add the fish bones, fish head, and parsley. Cook for 3 minutes, then add wine and 8 cups (1.9 liters) of water. Bring to a boil, then reduce to a simmer.

3 Cook for 1 hour, skimming as you go. DO not season!

4 Strain the stock in a fine-mesh sieve; you should have about 6 cups of clear fish stock.

5 In a ceramic heatproof pot on medium heat, combine the remaining 4 tablespoons (60 ml) oil, the remaining onion, and the saffron. Cook gently for 4 minutes, then add the rice and season with salt and pepper.

6 Cook the rice for 5 minutes, then add ¼ cup (60 ml) of the fish stock. Stir as you go with a wooden spoon. Continue adding the stock ¼ cup at a time until all the stock is absorbed and the rice is cooked al dente. This process will take about 35 minutes. Season and serve hot.

PASTA CARBONARA

SERVES 4

Sea salt
4 ounces (115 g) guanciale,
    sliced into thin strips
12 ounces (340 g) spaghetti
4 tablespoons (60 ml) olive oil
3 egg yolks, at room
    temperature
3 ounces (85 g) Pecorino
    Romano cheese, grated
Freshly ground black pepper

There are two myths to be dispelled about this dish at Barbuto. Number one: We do not use bacon. Number two, which I kinda love, is that even though it is only on the brunch menu, you can order it at any meal. The other pastas that we do this way are the bambini and the cacio e pepe.

The story of carbonara is shrouded in mystery. The usual narrative is that it was a coal miner's dinner, a hearty pasta after a miserable day in the mines, and the black pepper a memory of underground toils. Another story has it that in times past, when meat and fish were too expensive or not available, eggs were the best source of protein. So, a tiny bit of guanciale was cooked up, and then Grandma went chasing the eggs. The pasta went into the pot, the eggs were separated, and the guanciale was cooked in a good amount of oil. The eggs were added to the slightly warm pan, then pasta water was stirred into the egg-guanciale mixture, and then the pasta. Finally, some cheese, and voilà—pasta Carbonara!

1   Prepare a pot of boiling water with 1 teaspoon of salt.

2   In a large enameled saucepan, combine the guanciale and 3 tablespoons of olive oil. Cook for 5 minutes over a quiet flame.

3   Drop the pasta into the boiling water.

4   When the guanciale is golden, remove from the heat. Add the remaining olive oil.

5   Once the pasta is cooked, add the egg yolks to the pan with the guanciale, but don't mix them in yet!

6 Add ¼ cup (60 ml) of the pasta water to the pan and immediately, using a fork, gently incorporate the yolks, guanciale, and oil in the pan until homogenous but not curdled.

7 Drain the pasta and add it to the saucepan, stir well, and as you stir, sprinkle in the cheese.

8 Add 8 turns of black pepper from a pepper mill to the pasta and stir again. Serve hot.

PASTA CACIO E PEPE

10 ounces (280 g) spaghetti
2 tablespoons olive oil
3 tablespoons grated Pecorino
Romano cheese
1 tablespoon freshly ground
black pepper
4 tablespoons (55 g) butter

My first taste of cacio was when I was the chef at Michael's in Santa Monica in the early 1980s. Mauro Vincenti, the intrepid Italian restaurateur and Renaissance man, explained the dish. He told me three important things: first, the pasta has to be hot; second, you have to use the right amount of pasta water; and third, don't scrimp on freshly milled black pepper. Also, the right type of pecorino is essential. It really is the quintessential pasta; a little water, some well-cooked spaghetti, a handful of pecorino, and twenty turns of black pepper. Oh, and serve hot, please!

1   Bring a pot of salted water to a boil. Cook the spaghetti for 8–10 minutes, until al dente.

2   Drain and return to the pot, reserving ¼ cup (60 ml) of the pasta water.

3   Add the oil, cheese, and pepper to the spaghetti.

4   Add the pasta water and the butter and toss well. Serve.

CLAMS LINGUINI

2 pints (1 kg) Manila or\
    littleneck clams, scrubbed
1 cup (55 g) sliced ramps or
    scallions
½ cup (120 ml) white wine
2 cloves garlic
5 tablespoons butter
12 ounces (340 g) linguine
Sea salt
2 tablespoons chopped fresh
    chives
1 tablespoon fresh lemon juice

The best clams for this dish are from Puget Sound, unless you live in Italy, on the Adriatic, and can get some of the oval-shaped beauties called tellines. These are the most beautiful, expensive clams. I first tasted them in Venice at the restaurant da Fiore. They serve exquisite seafood in a romantic setting, perfect for a leisurely autumn meal. The tellines produce a briny, meaty taste. The Puget Sound Manila clams are quite briny and crisp as well, though not as elegant. The East Coast Manilas might be a bit big, so locate the smallest ones possible. Littleneck clams can work, but be careful of sand, bad clams, and broken shell fragments.

Where this dish can go south is if you overdo the wine or choose a wine that really doesn't work. I like Trebiano or Chasselas or Pinot Blanc, which do not have excess acidity or overripe fruit. They blend perfectly with the seawater in the clams. Also, don't overdo the butter!

1   In a saucepan, combine the clams, ramps, wine, garlic, and 1 tablespoon of the butter and cook over medium-high heat until the clams open. Discard any clams that have not opened.

2   Cook the pasta in boiling salted water for 7 minutes, then drain, reserving ⅓ cup (75 ml) of the pasta water.

3   When the clams are cooked, add the pasta and the reserved pasta water and toss well. Add the remaining 4 tablespoons butter.

4   Finish with the chives and lemon juice and serve.

PASTA POMODORO

SERVES 6 AS
A STARTER

FOR THE TOMATO SAUCE:

½ cup (120 ml) olive oil
1 medium onion diced (1 cup)
4 cloves garlic, smashed
1 cup (90 g) chopped leeks
1 cup (55 g) chopped scallions
1 glass (125 ml) prosecco
2 (28-ounce) cans or jars San
    Marzano tomatoes
1 cup (50 g) chopped fresh
    parsley
1 cup (40 g) chopped fresh
    basil
Sea salt

FOR THE PASTA:

12 ounces (340 g) dried pasta
2 tablespoons (85 g) butter
2 ounces (55 g) Parmesan
    cheese, grated

Luis Ruiz is one of my longtime line cooks; he is a master at producing ragù. I often think he instinctively knows how, because he has a great palate and perhaps his family taught everyone the basics of good Puebla, Mexico, cookery. We have evolved this recipe, and it keeps evolving. I am not the biggest fan of tomato concentrate (nor ketchup, for the same reason). It may have been invented by Escoffier, but I find it over-cooked, over-reduced, and it doesn't add freshness to anything.

We use great canned tomatoes: San Remo tomatoes from Italy or my friend Chris Bianco's from California. Chris adds some basil to his whole canned tomatoes, and that little bit makes a huge difference. The key here is to use a very heavy-bottomed stainless-steel or copper rondeau. A rondeau is expensive and hard to store, but it is truly unequaled in performance. The pan has a sandwich of copper and steel on the bottom, two convenient handles, and the perfect-sized sides. This ensures a great sauce or stew. The smallest rondeaus are perfect for the home; they hold 12 quarts and are very useful. *recipe continues*

Luis starts out sweating onions, garlic, and herbs in the rondeau with olive oil. If you want more flavor, add some minced guanciale, but then the whole vegetarian thing goes out the window. When the onions are tender, you can add the canned tomatoes, and the ragù begins. It is interesting how the sauce develops over time. We carefully and slowly simmer the tomatoes for about 4 hours, at a very low temperature, covered. While the tomatoes are cooking you can make meatballs, or the dessert, or something else.

The tomatoes transform in the rondeau, the flavor profile coalesces, and the sauce ripens. Toward the end you can add some seasoning and herbs.

1   Make the tomato sauce: In a heavy rondeau or casserole, combine the oil, onions, garlic, leeks, and scallions. Cook over medium heat for 10 minutes, or until golden.

2   Add the wine and cook for 10 minutes.

3   Add the tomatoes. Bring to a boil, stirring well, and then lower the heat to a simmer. Cover the pan and cook, for 2 hours, stirring every 10 minutes. Add the parsley and basil in the last 30 minutes. Remove the sauce from the rondeau and let cool then season with sea salt; do not strain!

4   Make the pasta: Cook the pasta in boiling salted water until al dente.

5   Heat 3 cups (480 ml) of the sauce in a saucepan with 2 tablespoons (55 g) butter.

6   When the pasta is cooked, drain, reserving 3 tablespoons (45 ml) of the pasta water, then toss it well with the sauce and cheese. Serve hot.

PASTA, SAUSAGE, AND BROCCOLI DI CICCIO

SERVES 4

Sea salt
2 tablespoons (60 ml) olive oil
2 cloves garlic
12 ounces (340 g) loose
    chorizo sausage
2 cups (140 g) sliced broccoli
    di ciccio
12 ounces (340 g) orecchiette
4 tablespoons (55 g) butter
2 tablespoons grated
    Parmesan cheese
¼ teaspoon red pepper flakes

A perennial seasonal favorite at Barbuto. Broccoli di ciccio has entered the mainstream in most supermarkets. It is considered a super-food, or something that tastes great and is actually good for you! It is a hardy, sturdy vegetable that loves abuse. It takes to flame or grill, high-temperature roasting, and will remain toothsome and nutritious. This pasta can be cooked in less than 20 minutes. Just have a pot for the pasta, another for the broccoli di ciccio, and a third for the chorizo sausage.

1   Prepare two pots of boiling, salted water.

2   In a saucepan, heat the oil and add the garlic and sausage; cook over medium heat for 10 minutes, stirring occasionally (it's okay if the chorizo sticks).

3   Drop the broccoli di ciccio into one of the pots of water. Drop the pasta in the other at the same time.

4   When the broccoli di ciccio is done, about 5 to 7 minutes, drain and add it to the chorizo, stir well to incorporate, turn up the heat, and add 2 tablespoons of the butter.

5   When the pasta is done, about 8 to 10 minutes, drain in a colander but reserve 3 tablespoons of the pasta water.

6   Add the reserved pasta water to the chorizo-broccoli mixture and mix well.

7   Finally add the pasta, the remaining 2 tablespoons butter, and the cheese, and season with red pepper flakes. Toss well and serve hot.

WHITE TRUFFLE RAVIOLI

SERVES 4

This is an easy luxury. The dough is half egg yolk, half flour; the filling is fresh ricotta and a smattering of white truffle. No herbs or mushrooms to clutter up the perfect ballet here. The truffle is, of course, a huge extravagance. So, check the truffle carefully to remove any dirt or sand. Then, using a sharp knife, carefully shave off the outer layer of the truffle. This will be the base for the filing. The remaining truffle will be shaved on a truffle slicer at the last minute.

Truffles vanish quickly, but the intoxicating odors that emanate from these exotic tubers are beyond description. Since they cost more than $250 per ounce, every bit counts. This dish will use about an ounce, so you want to ensure that the ones you buy are impeccable. Now the great part of this process is that one can substitute black truffles, summer truffles, and in a pinch, freshly bought Parisian mushrooms work very well (but they are not white truffles!).

6 ounces (115 g) fresh ricotta
8 tablespoons (1 stick/115 g)
     butter
1 white truffle (1 ounce/30 g)
Sea salt and freshly ground
     black pepper
4 sheets fresh pasta
3 egg yolks, beaten
2 tablespoons grated
     Parmigiano Reggiano

1   Put the ricotta in a bowl, add 4 tablespoons (55 g) of the butter, then grate in the outer part of the truffle; mix well and season with salt and pepper. Leave in the fridge overnight.

2   Make little raviolini: Brush the pasta sheets with the egg yolks. On the bottom sheet, place 1-ounce (28 g) dabs of the truffle mixture in rows every 2 inches (5 cm); lay the other sheet on top and press it into the bottom sheet to seal. Using a knife, cut out little squares of pasta with the filling.

3   Prepare a pot of boiling salted water. Cook the ravioli in the hot water until they float to the top, about 3 to 5 minutes; drain, reserving some of the pasta water.

4   In a saucepan, heat the remaining 4 tablespoons (55 g) butter until foaming, then add the ravioli and some of the pasta water.

5   Toss well, place on a platter, bring to the table, and slice the rest of the truffle on top. Finish with a dusting of Parmigiano Reggiano.

WILD BOAR PASTA

**SERVES 8
(WITH EXTRA RAGÙ)**

Wild boar is really popular near the town of Pitigliano, Italy. The boar must be plentiful in the area, because every restaurant serves a version. In America, we seem to have enclaves of wild boar; we do see a good population in California. One of my craziest memories of Philippe Jeanty, when we worked together at Domaine Chandon, was his fervent glee at receiving someone's hunt, a nice sixty-pound (27 kg) boar. He taught me the basics of butchery, and that has stuck.

On the Big Island in Hawaii, there are many feral pigs. There is a farmer who gets calls from frantic neighbors who have seen a good-sized boar rummaging around in the backyard. He hauls ass in his venerable Ford F150, lassoes the pig, shoves it in the pen, and brings it up to his farm at the base of Mauna Loa. There, he sets the pig loose in a pen with fellow vagrants. The macadamia nut farms are nearby, and due to a glitch in the production facility, a good amount of the nuts fall into a hamper below. The farmer scoops up these two-thousand-pound hampers, and those lucky pigs get a great last meal. If you can find some wild boar meat, go for it!

FOR THE PASTA:

12 large egg yolks
2 cups (250 g) organic all-
    purpose flour, plus more
    for dusting
½ teaspoon sea salt

FOR THE RAGÙ:

8 ounces (225 g) lean smoked
    ham, diced
2 tablespoons olive oil
2 onions, chopped
4 cloves garlic, smashed
Sea salt and freshly ground
    black pepper
1 pound (455 g) wild boar
    meat, cut into 1-inch (2.5
    cm) cubes (use pork butt
    if boar is not available)
1 pound (455 g) pork cheek
    meat, cut into 1-inch (2.5
    cm) cubes
1 (750 ml) bottle very cheap
    red wine
½ cup (25 g) chopped fresh
    Italian parsley
1 tablespoon grated fresh
    ginger
1 tablespoon grated lemon
    zest
1 teaspoon ground cumin
1 teaspoon ground turmeric
3 tablespoons butter
2 tablespoons grated
    Parmesan

1   Make the pasta: Put all the ingredients in the bowl of a stand mixer fitted with a paddle attachment and, on low speed, slowly bring the ingredients together into a rough ball. (You can also blend the ingredients in a food processor, just until they come together, to make the dough.) Transfer to a floured work surface and knead to form a nice, soft ball. Let the dough rest for 1 hour.

2   Cut the dough into two pieces. Roll out each piece as thin as you can manage. Dust each piece with flour, and roll each into a tight tube.

3   Using a sharp knife, cut ½-inch-wide (12 mm) fettuccini. Toss with flour and freeze.

4   Meanwhile, make the ragù: In a heavy saucepan, cook the ham with the oil over medium heat until slightly colored and cooked through. Add the onions and garlic, season well with salt and pepper, and cook until golden.

5   Remove all the ingredients from the pan and set aside, but leave the fat in the pot.

6   Add the boar and pork to the pot and season well, then cook over medium heat until deep brown. Deglaze the pan with the wine.

7   Return the ham and onion mixture to the pot, and add the parsley, ginger, lemon zest, cumin, and turmeric. Add 2 cups (720 ml) water, bring to a boil, cover, reduce to a simmer, and cook for 2 hours or until mushy. (This recipe makes enough sauce for about twelve portions of pasta.)

8   When cooked, taste the ragù for seasoning and stir in the butter.

9   Cook the frozen fettuccine in boiling salted water for 3½ minutes, then drain in a colander and return to the pot.

10   Add 3 cups of the boar ragù, and then the Parmesan. Toss well and serve.

DELICATA GNOCCHI

broccoli rabe and pepitas

SERVES 4 (WITH EXTRA GNOCCHI FOR THE FREEZER)

If there was one epiphany I have had while cooking, this was it. I had always felt let down by traditional gnocchi. I felt they were gummy or dry, never really perfect. I like to think that mistakes are simply the result of a bold gesture that went a bit haywire, and here is a perfect example. In the process of an elaborate dinner, I completely forgot to take the gnocchi out of the freezer. In a blind panic, I slapped a copper sauté pan on my home stove, threw on the gas, added some olive oil and whole butter. As the oil-butter sizzled in the pan, I tossed in the frozen gnocchi. I vigorously sautéed them, without understanding my endgame.

Finally, the gnocchi began to cook, and like little gummy bears, they squiggled about in the pan. As they turned brown and collected themselves, I tossed in some diced Jerusalem artichoke and some diced black truffle. Added a bit of water and then a knob of butter and a handful of grated Parmesan cheese. And guess what—magic!

So, we now complete one hundred to two hundred orders a day, and the process—frozen to cooked—remains. Good mistake, yes? *recipe continues*

FOR THE GNOCCHI:

Sea salt
4 medium russet potatoes
1 tablespoon olive oil
2 eggs, beaten
1½ cups (190 g) all-purpose
    flour

THE DISH:

3 tablespoons olive oil
3 tablespoons butter
1 cup (130 g) thinly sliced
    delicata squash (see Note)
1 cup (60 g) minced broccoli
    rabe
1 tablespoon pepitas (hull-less
    pumpkin seeds, usually
    from Syrian pumpkins;
    I use organic ones from
    Shiloh Farms)
2 tablespoons grated
    Parmesan cheese
1 tablespoon julienned fresh
    basil
Sea salt and freshly ground
    black pepper

*Note: To prepare the squash
    slices, cut a delicata in half
    and, using a spoon, scoop
    out the seeds; slice crosswise
    to make half-moons.*

1 Make the gnocchi: Boil the potatoes in simmering salted water for 45 minutes. Remove and let cool.

2 In a ricer, rice the potatoes, removing the peels as you go, onto a work surface. Sprinkle the riced potatoes with 1 tablespoon of the oil, 1 teaspoon salt, the beaten eggs, and flour.

3 Gently but quickly make a very tender dough and shape it into a mound. Cut the dough into six portions. Roll out each, one at time, into a rope ¾ inch (2 cm) thick. Cut into ¾-inch (2 cm) lengths and freeze the gnocchi for at least 2 hours or until ready to be used.

4 Cook the dish: In a large sauté pan, heat 1 tablespoon olive oil and 1 tablespoon butter; add 32 of the frozen gnocchi (yes, still frozen!). Let the gnocchi brown lightly, for about 5 minutes, turning to ensure that all sides get equal color. Remove the cooked gnocchi and keep warm.

5 Repeat step 4 with another 32 gnocchi. When cooked add to the first batch of gnocchi and keep warm.

6 In a large cast-iron pan, heat the remaining 1 tablespoon olive oil and 1 tablespoon butter over medium heat. Add the delicata squash and the broccoli rabe and sauté for 7 to 8 minutes, until golden.

7 Add the gnocchi to the squash and broccoli rabe, along with 2 tablespoons cold water and add 1 tablespoon butter. Toss well, add the pepitas, cheese, and basil, and season with salt and pepper; cook for 2 minutes. Serve hot.

CORN AND TOMATO GNOCCHI

SERVES 4

This recipe is for a special guest who admonishes me every time it is not on the menu (three hundred days a year!). I keep telling her to be patient, and the look on her face is of impatience and the bold hunger for this dish.

The technique here is worth the effort, truly! Start with medium-sized russet potatoes and cook them in gently simmering water flavored with sea salt and sage. When the potatoes are just cooked, they need to be cooled in the cooking liquid, and then the only method that works is to use a Mouli. This old-fashioned ricer is a terrific device for the best mashed potatoes, pureed carrots, and the making of gnocchi. The Mouli is quick, efficient, and a joy to use. The machine will fluff the potatoes so that when you add the flour, and egg, it will stay fluffy. The gnocchi get rolled out by hand.

At Barbuto, Martin, my pasta guru and an all-around good person, has very sure yet delicate hands. He doesn't rush the process, and he uses just a modicum of force when rolling out the dough. Gluten is the enemy here; too much elbow grease and the whole thing can go south. Freeze the gnocchi for a week, and the result will be perfect. When cooking, they are fairly elastic and will act a bit like Silly Putty; use a fork to nudge them around the pan. They take some time to brown, so be patient. *recipe continues*

2 tablespoons olive oil

3 tablespoons butter

64 frozen gnocchi (page 140)

2 cups (290 g) fresh corn
    kernels (from about 2 to
    3 cobs)

2 cups (290 g) cherry
    tomatoes, sliced

2 tablespoons butter

Sea salt and freshly ground
    black pepper

2 tablespoons grated
    Parmesan cheese

12 leaves of fresh basil

1   In a large heavy skillet, heat 1 tablespoon olive oil and
1 tablespoon of butter over medium heat; add 32 of the
gnocchi (yes, still frozen!). Let the gnocchi brown lightly, for
about 5 minutes, turning to ensure that all sides get equal
color. Remove the cooked gnocchi and keep warm.

2   Cook the rest of the gnocchi for 3 minutes, then add the
corn and tomatoes and return the previously cooked gnocchi to the pan.

3   Add the remaining 2 tablespoons butter and 2 ice cubes
to the pan; season with sea salt and pepper.

4   Add the cheese and the basil and cook for 2 minutes.
Serve hot.

GNOCCHI WITH ASPARAGUS AND MORELS

pesto and hazelnuts

SERVES 4

1 pound (455 g) morels
1 pound (455 g) asparagus
1 shallot, peeled and sliced
6 tablespoons (85 g) butter
4 tablespoons (60 ml) olive oil
¼ cup (60 ml) fino sherry
Sea salt and freshly ground
    pepper
64 frozen gnocchi (page 140)
3 tablespoons Hazelnut Pesto
    (page 251)
2 tablespoons hazelnuts

When the morels hit in spring, it is a joyous time at Barbuto. Morels are extraordinary. They are rich, flavorful, nutritious, and almost meat-like when cooked properly. They match perfectly with their garden cousins the asparagus. The pesto brings these two in perfect harmony and the hazelnuts are the crunch that adds that extra lagniappe.

1   Rinse the morels under cold running water; dry with a tea towel. Slice the morels in half or quarters if large.

2   Trim the base of each asparagus spear, and then slice the asparagus on the diagonal into 2-inch (5 cm) pieces.

3   In a large, heavy saucepan, combine the shallot, asparagus, and morels; add 1 tablespoon butter and 1 tablespoon olive oil.

4   Cook gently for 5 minutes. Add the sherry and reduce it until the pan is almost dry. Season the morels and asparagus with sea salt and pepper and then transfer them to a bowl.

5   In a heavy cast-iron pan, heat 1 tablespoon butter and 1 tablespoon olive oil over medium heat. Add half of the gnocchi (yes, still frozen!) and cook until golden brown on all sides; remove from the pan and keep warm.

6   Repeat with another tablespoon each of butter and oil and the other 32 gnocchi, and cook until golden.

7   Add the remaining 2 tablespoons butter and 2 ice cubes; season with sea salt and pepper.

8   Add the pesto and the hazelnuts. Toss well, season again, and serve hot.

PASTA BOLOGNESE

½ cup olive oil
1 pound (455 g) chopped beef
1 pound (455 g) chopped pork
1 pound (455 g) chopped veal
8 slices bacon, diced
Sea salt and freshly ground
    black pepper
Sea salt and freshly ground
    black pepper
2 onions, diced
1 head of garlic, roasted for 30
    minutes at 375°F (190°C)
    until soft
2 cups red wine
1 (28-ounce) can San
    Marzano tomatoes
1 bouquet garni (parsley,
    thyme, and bay leaf, tied
    with butcher's twine)
1 cup (240 ml) heavy cream
12 ounces pasta

Ah, Bolognese! I have eaten Bolognese at beloved restaurants in Modena, Bologna, and Milano. To say it is the go-to sauce of Emilia-Romagna is a gross understatement. Everyone has a favorite recipe or tip. I think the right balance of meats, coupled with the addition of tender, long-cooked onions and garlic, coupled with the exact amount of tomato, is the key. The most important gesture is long and slow, don't rush. Also, the sauce will freeze well; it tastes better after a sojourn in the refrigerator, and it loves a taste of heavy cream at the end, a sort of parting kiss.

1   In a large saucepan, about 12 inches in diameter, heat ¼ cup (120 ml) of the oil, all of the chopped meats, and the bacon. Season well with salt and pepper and cook until brown and crispy. Remove from the pan and set aside.

2   Add the remaining ¼ cup (120 ml) oil to the pan and the onions and garlic and cook until tender and golden.

3   Return the meat to the pan, along with the wine.

4   Cook until the wine is reduced to dry, then add the tomatoes, bouquet garni, and 2 cups water. Bring to a boil, then reduce the heat to a simmer, stir well, and cover. Cook gently for 2 hours or so, removing the cover halfway through the cooking time and stirring occasionally.

5   Add the cream and cook for 5 minutes. Remove from the heat. Remove the bouquet garni. Let cool slightly before serving with the pasta of your choosing.

ROCK SHRIMP PASTA

12 ounces (340 g) fresh pasta
   dough (see page 137),
   plus flour for dusting
Sea salt
1 tablespoon olive oil
3 tablespoons butter
1 pint (500 g) shelled fresh
   rock shrimp
2 tablespoons minced shallot
2 tablespoons diced Fresno
   chiles
2 tablespoons white wine
4 tablespoons (15 g) sliced
   scallions
1 teaspoon fresh lemon juice
Freshly ground black pepper

Ah, the chitarra, the most elegant and simplistic way to create extravagant pasta! The machine costs about thirty dollars, and it is handsome and makes for great kitchen decoration. It is so surprisingly fun and easy; you'll want to use it time and time again. And it will be a crowd-pleaser as well; everyone will want to try!

Rock shrimp are really prawns, but we call them shrimp. They have a seriously hard shell, which accounts for their spectacular flavor. They sauté beautifully and, of course, take to a deep-fry like a charm.

1   Roll the pasta dough out to $\frac{1}{16}$-inch thick. Cut into 12 by 6-inch (30.5 by 15 cm) sheets. Dust each sheet in flour, and then, one by one, firmly place the sheets on the top of the chitarra, and, using a rolling pin (a straight one without taper), push the pasta dough through the wires, and you will have magnificent chitarra noodles! (Note: You can also roll up the sheets; then cut strips $\frac{1}{8}$-inch thick to achieve a comparable noodle.)

2   Cook the pasta in boiling salted water for 4 to 5 minutes. Drain, reserving $\frac{1}{4}$ cup (60 ml) of the pasta water.

3   Heat a saucepan with the oil and 1 tablespoon of the butter over medium-high heat. Season the shrimp with salt and, when the butter, is foaming, sauté the shrimp for 3 or 4 minutes. Add the shallot and Fresno chiles.

4   Deglaze the pan with the wine and then add the remaining 2 tablespoons butter and the scallions. Add the reserved pasta water.

5   Season with the lemon juice and sea salt, plus freshly ground black pepper.

LEMON PASTA

edamame, Meyer lemon, and breadcrumbs

SERVES 4

3 tablespoons (55 g) butter
2 tablespoons olive oil
½ cup (25 g) fresh
      breadcrumbs
1 clove garlic, minced
Zest and juice of 1 Meyer
      lemon
1 tablespoon chopped fresh
      parsley
Sea salt
12 ounces (340 g) fresh
      tagliatelle
2 ounces (55 g) Parmesan
      cheese, grated
1 cup (75 g) cooked edamame

This is a wonderful and subtly exciting pasta. Its origins are tied to a dreamlike trip I took years ago to Positano, on the Amalfi Coast. The month of November is lemon time in Italy and especially so on the Amalfi. They use lemons in everything, but the best of all is with pasta.

For this pasta, gently grate the rind (only the yellow, avoid the white) and mix with the freshly squeezed juice. The pasta is tossed with a southern-style extra-virgin olive oil, minced garlic, and the lemon juice and zest. Then it is tossed with toasted breadcrumbs and edamame. Honestly, this is the paradigm of simplicity.

1   In a saucepan, heat 2 tablespoons of the butter and the oil over medium-high heat; add the breadcrumbs and sauté until golden, then add the garlic, lemon zest, and parsley. Mix well and season with salt.

2   Cook the pasta in boiling salted water until al dente, and then pour off all but ½ cup (120 ml) of the cooking liquid.

3   To the pasta, add the lemon juice, the remaining 1 tablespoon butter, and the cheese, mix well, and then add the breadcrumb mixture and the edamame. Toss well and serve hot!

COLLARD GREENS AND FARRO

leeks, fennel, and leaf parsley

SERVES 6

4 tablespoons (60 ml) olive oil
2 cups (110 g) chopped
    collard greens
2 leeks, washed and chopped
1 fennel bulb, diced
3 shallots, diced
Sea salt
1 cup (50 g) chopped fresh
    Italian parsley
4 tablespoons (55 g) butter
8 ounces farro
1 quart (960 ml) chicken stock

Collard greens are not a southern exclusive; in fact, we find them in many supermarkets. The great property of these wonderful greens is their intrinsic strength and ability to cook until they're tender and delicious. Farro, an ancient precursor to wheat, is a really toothsome grain. It has a terrific nutty quality and is very versatile. Here we cook it like risotto, and the result is a powerful dish that is hearty and filling but not clunky.

The tip is to cook the collards until tender. I find that adding water to the cooking pan helps set the water content, and this allows the olive oil to penetrate the greens and thereby provide them with the proper flavor profile.

1   In a heavy casserole, heat 2 tablespoons of the oil and add the collard greens, leeks, fennel, and shallots. Season with salt and cook slowly until soft and scrumptious. Add 1–2 cups water, cover, and cook on low for another 30–40 minutes.

2   Add the parsley and butter, gently toss to combine, and keep warm.

3   Toast the farro in the remaining 2 tablespoons oil, and then, using the chicken stock, cook like any risotto (see, for example, page 152) for about 30–35 minutes.

4   When cooked through, add the collard mixture, season with salt, and serve hot.

SHRIMP RISOTTO

SERVES 4

16 medium-sized fresh shrimp (save the shells and heads for the shrimp broth)
2 cups (500 ml) rosé wine
6 tablespoons (85 g) butter
1 small onion, diced
1½ cups (285 g) Arborio rice
Sea salt and freshly ground black pepper
2 tablespoons sliced Fresno chiles
2 cloves garlic, peeled
1 tablespoon each chopped fresh parsley, chives, and basil
1 tablespoon fresh lemon juice

A nice, comforting dish that smacks of flavor. The white wine and herbs balance the exciting taste of the clams, and the garlic is blanched first to ensure it is a flavor agent rather than the main event.

1   Make a shrimp broth: Place the shells and heads of the shrimp in 2 cups of the rosé wine and 2 cups cold water. Bring to a simmer and cook for 30 minutes, then strain.

2   In a heavy casserole, combine 1 tablespoon of the butter and the onion and sweat for 4 minutes, then add the rice. Season with salt and pepper now.

3   Add the remaining 1 cup wine and cook for 5 minutes.

4   Use the shrimp broth to form the risotto, adding one ladleful at a time to the rice mixture, until the liquid has been absorbed.

5   In a sauté pan, heat 2 tablespoons of the butter and cook the chiles and shrimp. Add ½ cup (120 ml) shrimp broth.

6   When the rice is almost cooked, add the shrimp mixture, then the herbs, the remaining 3 tablespoons butter, and the lemon juice. Season and serve hot.

SAUSAGE RAGÙ PASTA

fresh herbs, spinach, and ricotta

SERVES 4

2 tablespoons olive oil
1 pound (455 g) loose sausage,
    spicy or mild according to
    preference
1 onion, diced
4 cloves garlic, smashed
3 shallots, diced
4 fresh tomatoes, diced, or
    8 ounces (225 g) canned
    diced San Marzano
    tomatoes
1 cup (240 ml) red wine
10 ounces (280 g) pasta
Sea salt
1 tablespoon each chopped
    fresh parsley, basil, chives,
    and sage
11 oz (310 g) baby spinach
1 cup (240 ml) ricotta
2 tablespoons butter
Freshly ground black pepper

A nice dish for an autumn eve. The sauce is a quick ragù consisting of sausage (I like the spicy variety, but you can go with mild if you prefer). The spinach adds a fresh and colorful flavor that perks up the sausage. The tomatoes may be either fresh or canned; you can decide at the last minute.

1   In a heavy saucepan, heat the oil and sausage over medium heat and sauté until the sausage is really brown. Remove the sausage from the pan and set aside.

2   To the pan, add the onion, garlic, and shallots; cook for 5 minutes. Add the tomatoes and reintroduce the sausage. Add the wine. Cook until the wine has disappeared, then add the cold water. Bring to a boil, then lower the temperature. Cook for 30 minutes.

3   Cook the pasta in boiling salted water until al dente, drain, and add to the sausage mixture, along with the herbs and spinach and, at the last second, the ricotta.

4   Toss well, add the butter, and season with salt and pepper. Serve hot.

SPARE RIB RAGÙ PASTA

SERVES 4

2 racks baby back ribs
1 teaspoon sea salt, plus more
     to taste
1 teaspoon ground cumin
1 teaspoon fresh cracked black
     pepper
1 teaspoon smoked paprika
1 onion, peeled and left whole
3 cloves garlic, peeled and left
     whole
2 cups (480 ml) red wine
2 bay leaves
12 ounces (340 g)
     strozzapretti
1 tablespoon grated Pecorino
     Romano cheese
1 ounces (85 g) Parmesan
     cheese, grated
2 tablespoons butter

Here is a good example of using everything: One day I discovered my chefs had ordered so many ribs that it would be days before we could sell them all! What to do? I ordered the chefs to cook them on the bone, let them sit in the cooking liquid overnight, then the next day, strip the meat from the bone and make a rich sauce or ragù. And, of course, it was the best pork sauce anybody had ever tasted. So, from calamity to delight!

1   Preheat the oven to 400°F (205°C).

2   Rub the ribs with the salt, cumin, pepper, and paprika. Put in a roasting pan and roast until dark brown, about 1 hour. Lower the oven temperature to 375°F (190°C).

3   Add the onion, garlic, wine, 3 cups of water, and bay leaves to the roasting pan, cover, and continue to roast for 3 hours.

4   Remove the meat and scoop out the onions and garlic with a slotted spoon; let cool. When cool, remove the bones and discard.

5   Chop the meat and the onions and garlic, place in a saucepan and cook over low heat for 30–40 minutes, or until the liquid has reduced and everything is saucy.

6   Cook the pasta in boiling salted water until al dente and drain, reserving 3 tablespoons of pasta water. Place the pasta in a serving bowl, add 3 cups (720 ml) of the pork sauce, and toss well. Add both cheeses, the butter, and the 3 tablespoons of reserved pasta water and toss again. Season with salt and serve in the bowl.

BUCATINI ALL'AMATRICIANA

1 cup (225 g) diced guanciale
1 onion, minced
1 clove garlic, peeled and left
    whole
4 tablespoons (60 ml) olive oil
1 (8-ounce/225 g) can San
    Marzano tomatoes
12 ounces (340 ml) bucatini
Sea salt
3 ounces (85 g) Pecorino
    Romano cheese, grated
1 ounce (28 g) Parmesan
    cheese, grated

This is an old standby that we can't resist serving at Barbuto. The sauce is magic. There is a white version, which is essentially carbonara, and the red. Here we stick with the red one. The sauce originates from the town of Amatrice in Lazio, so one can go there to have the real item. There, they also do two versions, though I bet the red outsells the white four to one. Barbuto is a proud benefactor of these old recipes, but we also feel the need to make them our own. As you should as well.

1 In a heavy saucepan, combine the guanciale, onion, garlic, and oil. Cook gently over medium heat for 10 minutes, until golden in color.

2 Add the tomatoes and continue to cook for 20 minutes or until the sauce is flavorful and slightly thickened.

3 Cook the pasta in boiling salted water until al dente.

4 Drain, reserving 1 cup (120 ml) of the pasta water. Add the pasta and pasta water to the sauce.

5 Add the pecorino and toss to combine.

6 Season well with salt and serve in four bowls with a dusting of Parmesan.

FISH AND SEAFOOD

AS A CHILD GROWING UP in the Berkeley hills, one of my deep passions was fishing. I spent hours on the Berkeley pier. In the 1950s, the city of Berkeley pushed the pier almost a third of the way into the Bay, a bountiful fishing ground. We would pull in flounder, rockfish, sardines, and even a striped bass or two. I really did understand fish cookery as a child, and I enjoyed an occasional fish and chips. I loved Dungeness crabs from an early age. We would go on salmon fishing trips to the Farallon Islands off the coast of San Francisco, and there I would fish with my dad and brothers. I felt we were in another land, the sea churning about us and the seagulls squawking.

As I get older, I find myself eating almost an exclusively fish- and vegetable-based cuisine. I have always loved fish, from the trout I used to grill over the campfire, to fabulous fish and chips in London, to grilled Tasmanian lobsters in Australia and the ultimate: salmon coulibiac at Chez Panisse's New Year's celebration.

Fish has become my mantra, my salvation. Fish is a perfect protein; the only downside is that of scarcity and overfishing. Some fish are on the upswing, but statistics are not looking so good. I look at the Monterey Bay Aquarium Seafood Watch list often, and it does change ever so slightly. In any case, I feel better dining on fish, and I suppose my love of eating drives me to make good choices with fish.

I recently cooked a fish from my local farmer's market that is decidedly an overlooked varietal: pollock. I cooked it with what some of my colleagues might consider a culinary no-no—eggplant. However, the results shocked me. I guess the moral of the story is that no combination of ingredients should be ruled out. The succulent texture of the grilled eggplants coupled with the firm, but delicate pollock was delightful, and it came together in no time.

The fish we serve at Barbuto can come from as close as Fire Island or the Jersey Shore. I am so happy when we receive squeaky fresh fish that is literally off the boat. There is no greater pleasure than cooking a frisky soft crab, or a live shrimp from the Carolinas. From the magnificent striped bass to Montauk tuna, New York is an epicenter of the great catch. I adore the squid from Rhode Island, the fluke from Block Island, and the magnificent sea scallops from New Jersey.

I love wild salmon from California, Dungeness crab from the West Coast, king crab from Alaska, mussels from Prince Edward Island in Nova Scotia, and succulent lobsters from Maine. But it's the "trash" or bait fish that I truly adore: mackerel, sardines, little whitebait and the like; these are both sustainable and delicious. A sardine probably is the best fish that we can consume; they are laden with healthy nutrients and fabulous on the grill!

At Barbuto, we like a little heat with our fish or a good dose of citrus or garlic. Olive oil is simply indispensable, as is sea salt. The last is possibly the key ingredient. It makes any food pop, and fish especially.

WHOLE SEA BREAM

SERVES 4 TO 6

Bream is a magnificent fish. Firm, flaky when cooked well, the fish possesses a special flavor. The best way to preserve the taste of these great fish is cook them whole. Cooking whole really is not a hard thing to do. Practice, of course, makes perfect, but there are some good rules of thumb to follow. For every pound of fish, count 10 minutes for the first pound, then 8 minutes for each additional, up to 5 pounds. Once you get past 20 minutes, the heat becomes more efficient, so the cooking accelerates. So the math for a 3-pound (1.4 kg) fish is 30 minutes.

I adore the food of Liguria and the Italian Riviera. In Portofino, Genoa, and Cinque Terre, the food (and especially the seafood) is extraordinary. Talk about farm to table, this is the only methodology that they practice. One of the great local sauces is tapenade, the "caviar" of the Mediterranean. It is easy to make (or buy) and it is a universal sauce. At Barbuto, we use it indiscriminately, to great advantage. *recipe continues*

1 whole red snapper,
(3 pounds/1.4 kg),
descaled, gutted, and fins
trimmed

1 lemon, cut in half

1 cup plus 1 tablespoon
(240 ml) olive oil

Sea salt

1 bunch Swiss chard, leaves
and stems divided

6 tablespoons (85 g) butter

3 tablespoons white wine

3 cloves garlic, peeled, any
green sprouts removed

1 cup (155 g) pitted picholine
olives

Peel of 1 orange

1 tablespoon anchovy puree

1   Preheat the oven to 400°F (205°C).

2   Rub the fish with the lemon halves (reserve the lemon peel), some oil, and salt.

3   Mince the chard stalks and cook them in 1 tablespoon of the olive oil over medium heat until tender.

4   Toss the leaves of chard in 2 tablespoons of the oil and season with salt; make sure all the leaves are coated.

5   In a casserole rubbed with some of the butter, layer half of the Swiss chard leaves, and then lay the fish on top. Top with three pats of butter and then cover the fish with the remaining chard leaves. Sprinkle the leaves with some oil and the wine.

6   Bake for 30 minutes (see note above). Turn off the oven, and let fish rest in the oven while you make the tapenade. Leave it for at least 30 minutes.

7   In a food processor, pulse the garlic, olives, chard stems, the orange peel and reserved lemon peel, anchovy, and ¼ cup (60 ml) oil to a rough puree, then season the tapenade with salt.

8   Gently pull back the chard leaves and begin to serve the fish. It will be easy; just lift it out with a fork. Remove the head and backbone and continue to serve the fish.

9   Top each serving with the tapenade and garnish with chard leaves.

CIOPPINO, OR FISHERMAN'S STEW

SERVES 4 TO 6

The essence of any stew comprised of fish should be three things. One, a good mix of shellfish and whole fish; two, a base of onions, garlic, and perhaps fennel and/or ginger; and three, vegetables that will be hardy enough to stand up to a long cook. This recipe has these three components. I love the mix of shrimp, clams, mussels, cod, and squid. These all have their intrinsic flavors; however, together they really begin to shine. Fennel is a strong root vegetable that is an exemplary building block for a good stew. A good stewing vessel is important, and some grilled bread helps finish the dish in a grand manner. *recipe continues*

2 cups (480 ml) good rosé
    wine
4 fresh parsley stems
1 pound fish bones
1 jalapeño chile, seeded and
    minced
1 onion, chopped
4 fingerling potatoes, diced
4 cloves garlic, thinly sliced;
    plus 1 clove peeled and
    halved
1 fennel bulb, chopped
Pinch of saffron
1 pound (455 g) cleaned
    squid, left whole if
    possible
1 pound (455 g) Puget Sound
    mussels, scrubbed
1 pound (455 g) Manila
    clams, scrubbed
1 pound (455 g) Santa
    Barbara prawns, left
    whole, head on
⅓ cup (55 g) pitted picholine
    olives
2 heirloom tomatoes, cored
    and cut into large cubes
4 (5-ounce/180 g) cod fillets
2 tablespoons olive oil
1 baguette, split in half
    lengthwise
Sea salt and freshly ground
    black pepper
2 tablespoons chopped fresh
    parsley

1   Make a fish broth: In a small stockpot, combine 1 quart (960 ml) water, the wine, and parsley. Bring to a boil, add the fish bones, and cook for 1 hour. Strain through a fine-mesh sieve, discarding the bones.

2   In a large stockpot with a lid, combine the fish broth, jalapeño, onion, potatoes, sliced garlic, and fennel. Add the saffron and squid. Cover and cook over medium heat until the vegetables are al dente and the squid are stewed, about 10 minutes.

3   Add the mussels, clams, prawns, olives, and tomatoes. Bring to a boil, then reduce to a simmer and cover. Cook for 5 to 8 minutes, until the mussels and clams have opened.

4   In a saucepan, heat 1 tablespoon oil on medium heat. Add the cod fillets and cook until medium. Keep warm.

5   Meanwhile, grill the baguette over medium-high heat in a grill pan, rub the cut sides with the halved garlic clove and the olive oil.

6   Season the cioppino with salt and pepper and divide the stew among four bowls. Top each serving with a cod fillet and garnish with parsley.

PAN-ROASTED TILEFISH

corn, tomatoes, edamame, and red onion

SERVES 4

2 ears of corn, in their husks
4 (4-ounce/170 g) tilefish
     fillets
Sea salt and freshly ground
     black pepper
4 tablespoons (55 g) butter
1 red onion, diced
½ cup (65 g) cooked
     edamame
2 heirloom tomato, stemmed
     and diced
Juice of 1 lemon

Many years ago, tilefish were commonly served in coastal areas along the Gulf of Mexico and the Atlantic coast south of Delaware. Tilefish are very firm, dense, and meaty. They cook well and are flaky and rich. The best method to cook these marvelous fish is to pan roast them. This technique works well with dense fish, forcing them to release their intrinsic flavors and at the same time rendering the meat tender and delicate.

1   Preheat the oven to 375°F (190°C). Place the ears of corn with their husks on a sheet pan sprinkled with ¼ cup cold water. Cook for 40 minutes. Remove and let cool.

2   Season the fish with salt and pepper. In a sauté pan, heat 2 tablespoons butter to a sizzle. Add the tilefish and cook, skin side down, for 3 minutes, flip over, and cover the pan. Cook for 4 minutes.

3   Remove the tilefish and add 2 tablespoons of the butter and the red onion to the pan.

4   Shuck the corn and slice the kernels off the cobs. Add to the onions in the pan. Cook for 8 minutes over medium heat.

5   Add the edamame and tomatoes. Season with salt and pepper. Stir well and add the lemon juice.

6   Cook for 5 minutes, then reintroduce the tilefish to gently rewarm it.

7   Scoop the contents onto a large platter and serve hot.

GRILLED SOFT-SHELL CRABS

SERVES 4

4 soft-shell crabs, cleaned and prepared by your fishmonger

4 tablespoons (60 ml) olive oil, divided

1 teaspoon plus 1 tablespoon fresh lemon juice

1 teaspoon coarse cracked black pepper

4 organic cucumbers, in their peels, washed

Sea salt

1 cup purslane

1 shallot, minced

I love soft-shells. They are such a treat when they come into season. We harvest them from three distinct areas. The first to begin the molting process are in Louisiana; we might see some "buster" crabs as early as March or April. The second wave come from the intercoastal area from Georgia up to Virginia. These crabs are very different from their gulf cousins, less fatty, crisper, and perhaps livelier. Last, we get the bumper crop from the Chesapeake. These guys are favorites, frisky and quite delicious when grilled. Grilling is a great method for crabs tossed in some olive oil and lemon. They cook in a heartbeat, so be careful!

1   Marinate the crabs in 1 tablespoon of the oil, 1 teaspoon of the lemon juice, and the black pepper for 1 hour.

2   Prepare a charcoal grill or heat a gas grill to medium.

3   Cut the cucumbers in half lengthwise and season with salt and oil.

4   Grill the cucumbers until cooked, about 3 minutes per side, then let cool.

5   Chop the cucumbers and toss them in a large bowl with the remaining 1 tablespoon lemon juice and 1 tablespoon olive oil, the purslane, shallot, and salt to taste.

6   Grill the crabs on each side for 3 to 5 minutes.

7   When cooked, place the crabs shell side up on a platter and serve with the cucumbers.

SWORDFISH WITH TOMATO-CUCUMBER SALSA

SERVES 4

2 (12-ounce/340 g) swordfish
    steaks
6 tablespoons (90 ml) olive oil,
    divided
Sea salt and cracked black
    pepper
3 lemon cucumbers, washed
3 medium-sized heirloom
    tomatoes
2 cloves garlic, minced
2 shallots, minced
1 Fresno chile, seeded and
    minced
12 fresh mint leaves
12 sprigs of watercress

Swordfish is a magnificent game fish that cooks perfectly. It can be grilled or sautéed, but grilling is truly the best method. It seals in the juices, adds some spectacular umami flavor, and is fun to do as well. There are no real tricks to swordfish—it cooks quickly and is hard to cook badly. I like to season it, add some olive oil, and simply grill it like a steak, over some good heat.

The tomato salsa needs some bright, ripe heirlooms to work well. I like the round yellow lemon cucumbers; they are hardy, have small seeds, and are a good partner to the tomatoes. Add some Fresno chile, shallots, olive oil, and garlic, and you are all set!

1   Prepare a grill to medium heat.

2   Season the swordfish with 4 tablespoons (60 ml) of the oil, salt, and cracked pepper.

3   Make the salsa: Dice the cucumbers and tomatoes and place in a bowl; add the garlic, shallots, and chile. Add the remaining 2 tablespoons oil and toss to combine. Season with salt and cracked pepper.

4   Grill the swordfish, about 6 minutes per side. Set upon a large platter, add the salsa, and garnish with the mint and watercress. Serve hot.

RED SNAPPER

black and red lentils

SERVES 4

4 (4-ounce/115 g) red snapper
    fillets, skin on
Olive oil
Sea salt
½ cup beluga lentils
½ cup red lentils
2 cloves garlic
2 tablespoons butter
Juice of 1 lemon
2 tablespoons chopped fresh
    parsley stems

Properly sourced red snapper is truly a wonderful product, perhaps the best fish in Florida.

1   Rinse the fillets and pat dry. Rub with olive oil and season with sea salt.

2   Put the lentils in two small pots (one type in each pot). To each pot, add 1 clove garlic, 1½ teaspoons butter, and 1 teaspoon sea salt, along with 1¼ cups cold water.

3   Cook the lentils gently until tender, about 30 minutes. There should be no liquid left. Keep the lentils in their pots.

4   In a large cast-iron skillet, add 1 tablespoon olive oil and the remaining 1 tablespoon butter.

5   Heat to sizzling and add the fillets, skin side down. Cook for 3 minutes.

6   Turn over the fillets and turn off the heat. Cover and let sit for 5 minutes.

7   Add the juice of 1 lemon to the red snapper pan and then mix the beluga and red lentils together. Place the lentils and red snapper on a platter.

8   Top with the parsley and sprinkle with olive oil and sea salt.

STRIPED BASS STEAK

broccolini, anchovy, and brown butter

SERVES 4

4 (5-ounce) striped bass steaks
Sea salt and freshly ground
    black pepper
2 tablespoons olive oil
3 cups broccolini florets
1 tablespoon anchovy paste
5 tablespoons (45 g) butter
1 tablespoon apple cider
    vinegar
1 clove garlic

I just love striped bass. When I was growing up in the San Francisco Bay Area, stripers were the ultimate catch. Little did I realize how foreign they were to the waters of the East Coast. Introduced by intrepid fishing enthusiasts, the striped bass have flourished. The version in the Chesapeake are called "rock fish"; they are smaller than the monsters my friends catch out near Montauk, in Long Island.

The striped bass is a fighting fish, so the flesh is not delicate, but firm and with an almost meat-like complexity. It lends itself to grilling; and the skin, which some folks find a mite too strong, has a dense, salty quality that tastes like the sea and I assume is very nutritious as well. Broccolini is soooo Italian, and the striped bass is reminiscent of its Mediterranean cousin the branzino. Together, these ingredients scream Italy.

1   Season the bass fillets with salt and pepper.

2   In a heavy skillet, heat 1 tablespoon of the oil over high heat. Add the broccolini and sauté for 3 minutes. Add the anchovy paste and 2 tablespoons (28 g) butter and toss to coat the broccolini. Season with sea salt. Remove from the pan and keep warm.

3   Wipe the pan with a paper towel. Add 1 tablespoon butter and the remaining 1 tablespoon oil. When foaming, add the fillets, skin side down, and cook until golden brown on the skin side, about 5 to 6 minutes. Remove the fish and place on a warm platter.

4 In the same pan over high heat, add the vinegar and garlic and use a whisk to scrape up the pan juices. Lower the heat to medium and add the remaining 2 tablespoons (28 g) butter; whisk the butter into the vinegar and pan juices.

5 Spoon the sauce over the fish, garnish with the broccolini, and serve.

PARCHMENT-BAKED COD

heirloom tomatoes

SERVES 4

4 (4-ounce/115 g) thick cod
    fillets
Sea salt
2 heirloom tomatoes, stems
    removed, diced
2 cloves garlic, slivered
1 shallot, sliced
8 fresh basil leaves
2 tablespoons olive oil, plus
    more for the parchment
2 tablespoons butter

Parchment cooking helps with foods that can lose their mojo while roasting in an oven or on the grill. It preserves the moistness of the contents, has an amazing ability to meld all the ingredients together into a fine web of flavor, and it is totally easy.

At Barbuto, I love this dish for lunch. Everyone is happy to receive the roasted, toasty, puffy culinary present in a dish. Waiters are happy to open the bag at the table and allow the amazing odors trapped by the parchment to waft over to the guest.

1   Preheat the oven to 375°F (190°C). Prepare four 8 by 12-inch (20 by 30.5 cm) pieces of parchment.

2   Season each fillet with sea salt.

3   Toss the tomatoes with the garlic, shallot, basil, and oil.

4   Oil the four rectangles of parchment and fold each one in half the long way to create a crease. Open up the parchment, put a fillet on one-half of each piece, and one-fourth of the tomato mixture on top of each fillet. Dot each fillet with 1½ teaspoons butter and season with more sea salt.

5   Fold each rectangle in half over the fish and place them on a baking sheet. Then fold over the corners to tightly seal. Brush the tops of the parchment with oil.

6   Bake for 6 to 8 minutes. You can test the fish by using a probe thermometer; it should read 140 degrees or more. This is really a guide, not a perfect science. Remove from the oven. Let rest for 5 minutes.

7   Serve each pouch on a plate; have each guest cut open his or her envelope.

BAKED HAKE

SERVES 4

4 (5-ounce/140 g) hake fillets
Sea salt and freshly ground
    black pepper
4 tablespoons (60 ml) olive oil,
6 tablespoons (70 g) plus 4
    teaspoons (18 g) butter
3 ounces (85 g) breadcrumbs
6 medium leeks
1 tablespoon fresh lemon juice
8 fresh sage leaves

"Hake" is a lukewarm name for anything, and for a fish, it is downright mundane. Yet the lowly name describes a beautiful fish. It is flaky yet surprisingly rich, delicate and yet almost dense. It is also very fragile and does not keep for long. Here is a great way to explore the pleasures of this fish. The breadcrumbs add flavor, richness, and crunch. The leeks are a perfect companion; the emulsified butter sauce adds a robe of flavor and richness that allows the hake to stand out. A judicious amount of sage adds mystery and excitement.

1   Preheat the oven to 375°F (190°C). Season the hake with sea salt and pepper and rub with 2 tablespoons of the oil.

2   In a sauté pan, heat 2 tablespoons butter and sauté the breadcrumbs until golden. Season the fish with salt and pepper

3   Wash the leeks and cut off the tops and ends. Cut in half lengthwise and wash in cold water to remove any sand.

4   Bring a large pot of salted water to a simmer. Cook the leeks until tender, about 10 minutes.

5   Place the fillets in a buttered casserole dish and top each with 1 teaspoon of butter. Place the leeks around the fish and bake in the oven for 10 to 12 minutes.

6   Meanwhile, make a butter sauce: In a small saucepan, add 3 ice cubes, 4 tablespoons butter, and 1 tablespoon lemon juice. Heat over a low flame and whisk continuously; the sauce should emulsify. Season with sea salt and pepper.

7   Divide the hake among four plates and top with breadcrumbs and butter sauce. Garnish with leeks and 2 sage leaves per plate.

CAPESANTE

sea scallops, cranberry beans, Sungold tomatoes, and chives

SERVES 4

12 large scallops
Sea salt and freshly ground
    black pepper
1 tablespoon olive oil
2 tablespoons butter
½ cup (65 g) cooked
    cranberry beans
½ cup (75 g) fresh corn
    kernels
1 shallot, minced
½ cup (90 g) sliced Sungold
    tomatoes
1 tablespoon fresh lemon juice
2 tablespoons pitted green
    olives
1 tablespoon minced fresh
    chives

The diver scallops we purchase for Barbuto are starting to be seen in various markets around the U.S. They must travel well, or perhaps they are flash frozen and then thawed. They actually take to freezing better than most other seafood. I would rather buy them frozen and let them defrost in my refrigerator.

The best tip for these beauties is to cook them on one flat side for about 75 percent of the required cooking time. The side cooking will transfer some of the heat through the scallop, and the reverse side will begin to sweat. When you turn the scallops over, that sweat transforms into beautiful caramelization.

1   Season the scallops with salt and pepper.

2   Heat a skillet, add the olive oil, and heat until smoking. Tilt the pan and using a pair of tongs, gingerly place all the scallops in the pan, flat side down. Cook until brown on one side only, about 3 minutes. Flip the scallops over and cook for 1 minute only! Remove from the pan.

3   Add the butter to the pan, then add the beans, corn, and shallots and cook for 2 minutes; add the tomatoes. Add the lemon juice and olives. Remove from the heat and season.

4   Add the scallops back to the pan. Turn on the heat for 2 minutes and toss well.

5   Divide among four plates and garnish with chives.

BROILED CHAR WITH CHANTERELLES

SERVES 4

I am a lover of all things salmon. Smoked, tartar, carpaccio, skewers, raw, cooked, and cured. It is a fish that could help save your life. In the wild form, from Alaska, the omega-3 fats in the fish are a great deterrent to heart disease. In fact, many folks prescribe salmon as an essential part of the diet to recover from heart procedures. I am also a fan of salmon skin. Especially when it is grilled or broiled. Not to everyone's taste, but I adore it.

Land-locked salmon or char might be some of the tastiest fish I have ever eaten. Char is as healthy as salmon, but has a delicateness, a silkiness; it is perhaps less fishy than its big cousin. It is a versatile fish, and it can be served, like salmon, in many different ways.

Here is an elegant dish that is extremely fast to make. From start to finish this dish will take fifteen minutes—not bad for a busy lifestyle! The ingredients are great on their lonesome, but when you combine chante-relles with char, the flavors begin to explode. I love to serve a Condrieu with this dish. The wine of a tiny appellation on the Rhône river in France lends a delicious, almost anise-like, note. *recipe continues*

4 (5-ounce/140 g) boneless
    char fillets, skin on
Sea salt and cracked black
    pepper
5 tablespoons (70 g) butter
2 shallots, thinly sliced
1 clove garlic
8 ounces (225 g) chanterelle
    mushrooms
3 tablespoons chopped fresh
    parsley

1   Season the char with salt and cracked pepper.

2   Butter a broiler-proof ceramic oval baking dish with 1 tablespoon of the butter and lay the fish in the dish skin side up. Butter the skin lavishly with 2 tablespoons of the butter.

3   In a sauté pan, combine the shallots, garlic, and remaining 2 tablespoons butter. Cook over medium heat for 5 minutes, then add the chanterelles. Cook for another 5 minutes, then stir in the parsley.

4   Heat the oven to broil (500°F/260°C). Place the fish in the baking dish under the broiler for 8 minutes.

5   Remove the fish from the oven. Garnish with the chanterelle sauce. Serve hot in the ceramic dish.

TROUT WITH TOASTED HAZELNUTS

SERVES 4

2 cups (255 g) all-purpose
    flour
1 cup (180 g) finely milled
    cornmeal
Sea salt
1 cup (240 ml) milk
1 egg
4 small trout (complete with
    bones and head)
10 tablespoons (1½ sticks)
    butter
4 tablespoons (60 ml) olive oil,
    plus more if needed
2 ounces (55 g) hazelnuts,
    crushed
1 tablespoon fresh lemon juice

Nothing is better than a freshly caught trout, yet nothing is worse than a sad, defrosted trout, sitting in the supermarket fish case pleading for some fool to buy it.

You will know a fresh trout. Their eyes will be vibrant and clear, the bodies almost stiff. They will smell of basically nothing and have squeaky skin. This recipe is a gold standard in fish cookery. I like to use an oval copper pan, which holds the fish nicely.

1   Put 1 cup (125 g) of the flour in a paper bag with the cornmeal and season with salt.

2   Whisk the milk and egg together. Season as well.

3   Dip a trout into the milk and egg mixture for 5 minutes.

4   Add one trout to the paper bag, shake well to coat, then place the trout on a plate. Repeat with the remaining trout.

5   In an oval fish pan or large sauté pan or skillet, combine 4 tablespoons (55 g) of the butter and the olive oil over medium-high heat. Cook 2 trout until golden brown on one side, then flip them over and cook the other side. Keep warm on a serving platter.

6   Repeat with the remaining trout; add more butter and oil if necessary.

7   Add 2 tablespoons butter to the pan and add the hazelnuts. Cook for 3 minutes until toasted and add the lemon juice.

8   Drizzle over the trout and serve hot.

SALLY'S BIRTHDAY PAELLA

SERVES 8

2 pounds (910 g) fresh shrimp (peeled; save the shells)
1 pound (455 g) fish heads
2 glasses rosé wine
2 bay leaves
1 bunch fresh parsley
2 (1¼-pound/570 g) Maine lobsters
2 tablespoons (30 ml) olive oil
6 chicken thighs (boneless, skin on), cut in half
Sea salt and freshly ground black pepper
1 cup (225 g) diced Spanish chorizo
1 onion, diced
2 cloves garlic, thinly sliced
2½ cups (475 g) Arborio rice
1 teaspoon smoked paprika
2 pinches of saffron
1 pound (455 g) bass or rock cod fillet (skin on), cut into 2-ounce (55 g) pieces
Aioli (page 249)

My wife is a Leo. She loves Barbuto with a passion unlike anyone I know. But when it is time to celebrate her birthday, our family is usually in France, in the Haute-Savoie. And this is what I make for her. The house we visit is nestled in the cradle of an amazing mountain called La Tournette. Sally loves to climb up this steep beast of a mountain and then to enjoy paella as her birthday reward on her return.

1   Make a shrimp, fish-head, and lobster broth: Put the shrimp shells, fish heads, wine, and 2 cups (480 ml) cold water in a pot and bring to a boil.

2   Add the bay leaves and parsley. Cook for 45 minutes. Strain and bring to a boil again.

3   Place the lobsters into the broth and cook for 7 minutes. Remove and let cook, then deshell the lobsters. Place the lobster shells into the broth, bring to a boil, and cook for 30 minutes. Put the lobster meat into the refrigerator. Strain the broth; discard the shells.

4   In a 20-inch (50 cm) paella pan over an outdoor grill or two gas burners, heat the oil over medium heat. Season the chicken with salt and pepper and add it with the chorizo to the pan; cook the thighs skin side down until golden brown, 10 minutes. Turn over the chicken and add the onions and garlic. Cook for 5 minutes, then add the rice.

5   Cook the rice for 5 minutes, stirring constantly. Add 4 cups (900 ml) of the broth and cook for 5 minutes. Add the paprika, saffron, bass, shrimp, and lobster meat.

6   Bring to a boil and then lower the heat to a rolling simmer. Add more broth if too dry; do not stir! Cook for 20 minutes, then remove from heat. Serve with aioli.

WHOLE STEELHEAD

greens and lemon

SERVES 8

4 pounds (1.8 kg) rock salt
4 egg whites
1 (3- to 4-pound/1.4 to
   1.8 kg) steelhead trout
2 cups (450 g) picked,
   washed, and dried mixed
   greens (collard, chard,
   spinach, etc.)
1 clove garlic, smashed
3 shallots, sliced
2 tablespoons olive oil
Sea salt
2 lemons, quartered

The best game fish is a steelhead. When you hook one, the fight is tremendous, which is probably why steelheads taste so good. The flesh is a vibrant shade of orange-red and it is delicate and meaty at the same time. Steelhead season usually lasts about two months in California, and the fishermen (many from local native tribes, who make their year's wage tackling this very hard job) bring a meager amount to the marketplace.

The difference between a wild steelhead and domesticated salmon is light-years. Especially cooked whole, these magnificent creatures bring out all the great things about being a chef: respect for the fishermen, the ultimate reverence for the product, and a sense of responsibility to cook the fish with skill and passion.

1   Preheat the oven to 400°F (205°C).

2   Mix the rock salt and egg whites with a wooden spoon. Place one-third of the rock salt mixture on a baking sheet. Place the fish on top. Cover the fish with the remaining rock salt. Bake for 45 minutes. Remove from the oven and let sit.

3   In a sauté pan, cook the greens in the oil with the garlic and shallots for 4 minutes, until wilted. Season the greens with sea salt.

4   Gently lift off the rock salt from the fish and remove the skin of the fish. Scoop out the meat onto eight plates, dividing it equally, and garnish each serving with the greens and a quarter of a lemon.

POULTRY

IT HAS BEEN NOTED by some that I cook a good bird. I suppose there are a number of factors that support this statement. Perhaps the most important is the simple truth of hours. I have devoted so much time to bird cookery that it has become a part of me.

There are, of course, many ways to cook poultry; I love poaching, which is delicious and perhaps slightly out of favor in today's kitchens. Grilling is my absolute favorite method, and, yes, sautéing is great, albeit a bit tricky. Lastly, stewing, which is a really perfect technique for birds. Whatever method makes sense at the moment. I suggest you try them all! There are other types of poultry cookery: salt crusted, baked in clay, baked in banana leaves, etc., but for the most part these seem outside the realm of Barbuto.

I wooed my wife on a poached chicken, I made my reputation on a grilled one, and I like to roast them at home. And if I am blue, a stew it is!

Stewing is an art. The chicken, duck, or squab needs some careful butchery to achieve perfect results. Also, one should not underseason a stew. Too often stews are started too early or too late, and the result can be strange or boring. To prepare a proper stew, you should be careful with your choice of ingredients. It truly matters whether to use garlic or ginger or wine or herbs. The flavoring agents will make all the difference in the end result.

It is important to remember to finish a stew with a jolt of fresh flavor, a bit of pesto, a dash of cream, perhaps a bit of chile; all of these will help bring out the flavor.

Grilling is our national pastime. I grew up (as did many of you) with a standard backyard grill and the ubiquitous charcoal briquettes. Over the years I have cooked over campfires at 10,000 feet in altitude, on gas grills in luxurious homes where the grill had never been used, on a tiny hibachi on a porch in Topanga Canyon, and of course in an indoor fireplace or two. No matter what the grill is made of, the same technique and advice ring true. When cooking poultry on the grill, your flame cannot be too high (or too low for that matter).

Poultry likes a subtle fire that has cooled a bit from the full blast. Some patience is necessary. You need to babysit while cooking at the grill. You can't wander off to play music or to make a cocktail. The grill could be your favorite device; however, you need to embrace its limitations. Also, ladies and gents, your grill needs to be cleaned!

Roasting birds might be the most bulletproof method. I have used tabletop miniature ovens, massive, electric deck ovens, commercial convection ovens, newfangled combi ovens, and good old-fashioned gas ovens. Regardless of the source, here are a couple of tips: preheat the oven for a minimum of an hour; this is really a prerequisite. Use an oven thermometer to determine the true temperature of your oven. Use cooking gloves made of leather (welder's gloves are cheap and perfect). Don't be afraid of your oven—it can and should be your best friend! Lastly, make sure the oven is clean. Old fish and meat juices can permeate the oven and lend an off note to those delicate birds. Final word of advice: Baste your bird like a pro!

JW CHICKEN

salsa verde

SERVES 4

1 (3½-pound/1.6 kg) free-range organic chicken (fresh not frozen)
Sea salt and freshly ground black pepper
¼ cup (60 ml) extra-virgin olive oil
Salsa Verde (page 250)

This is the cornerstone of Barbuto. At last count, we have served about 350,000 orders of my chicken! It is a testament to the bird (a Lancaster County farm-raised bird from Bell & Evans), the oven designed by Nobile, and our customers, who "flock" to Barbuto to eat this chicken.

Of course, the cooking is the really important part of the puzzle. The method is simple: Cut the chicken in half and remove the backbone. Next, cut off the wings so that only the little drumstick is attached. Next, carefully carve out the breastplate. The next step is to rub with olive oil, and then sprinkle with salt and fresh black pepper. We do not brine the birds as others are wont to do.

Because the chicken has lost some weight in the butchering process, cooking time is vastly reduced, no more than half an hour.

1   Preheat the oven to 450°F (230°C).

2   Remove the bird from the plastic wrap and discard any bag juice.

3   Pat dry with paper towels.

4   Place the chicken, breast side down, on a cutting board. Using poultry shears, cut along both sides of the backbone; remove and discard the backbone. Remove any fat (this can be added to a chicken stock). Using a heavy chef's knife, cut out the breastbone. Season the two halves with salt and pepper. *recipe continues*

5   Place the chicken halves, skin side up, in a roasting pan coated with oil and dab with more oil. Roast the chicken for 30 minutes, basting every 10 minutes. If it is not browning well, turn it over after 15 minutes, and then right it for the last 5 minutes.

6   When it is done, remove the chicken to a platter and pour off the excess fat. Let rest for at least 30 minutes.

7   To serve, place the bird back in the oven for 5 to 8 minutes. Remove and cut the bird into serving pieces: Cut each breast in half and cut the thighs from the legs, serve with salsa verde.

DUCK, PEAS, AND MORELS

ramps

SERVES 4

1 (4-pound/1.8 kg) fresh duck, preferably Bell & Evans
Sea salt
1 onion, sliced
2 carrots, peeled and diced
4 cloves garlic
1 stalk celery, diced
Bouquet garni (parsley, thyme, and bay leaf tied together with butcher's twine)
3 tablespoons butter
1 cup (110 g) morel mushrooms, washed and cut in half
2 cups (290 g) freshly shelled peas
1 small bunch (about 1 cup) ramps, washed and trimmed

This is a great culinary trio. It is obviously a spring dish; if you are inclined to cook this in another season, use porcini and romanesco in autumn, leeks and chard in the winter, and peppers in the summer.

There is a poultry farm owned by Bell & Evans that produces a delicious Long Island–style duck. The ducks weigh about 4 pounds, and they roast wonderfully. I like the method I learned years ago from Jean-Pierre Moullé of Chez Panisse: Roast the duck in the oven at a high temperature. Baste vigorously, and then let rest for 1 hour. This yields a beautiful, parchment-like skin, succulent meat, and bones that make for a wonderful duck jus.

This recipe is very approachable and will please everyone.

1   Preheat the oven to 425°F (220°C).

2   Rub the duck with salt. Place in a roasting pan breast side up with ½ cup (120 ml) water and roast for 1 hour. Baste the duck every 15 minutes. Shake the pan so the duck does not stick.

3   Meanwhile, prepare a court bouillon: Put the onion, carrots, garlic, celery, bouquet garni, and 2 quarts (2 L) water in a pot and bring to a boil. Lower the heat to a simmer and cook for 1 hour.

4   When the duck is cooked, remove from the pan and let sit for 1 hour. Deglaze the roasting pan and add the pan juices to the court bouillon. *recipe continues*

5 Carefully cut off the breast meat and pull off the legs and thighs. Put in the refrigerator until ready to use.

6 Place the duck carcass in the court bouillon and cook for 3 hours.

7 Strain the stock through a fine-mesh sieve, discard the solids, then cook over high heat to reduce until 2 cups (480 ml) remain.

8 Set a saucepan with duck sauce, add the cooked thighs and legs. Cook at a simmer for 15 minutes or until tender at the bone.

9 When cooked through, remove the thighs and legs from the pan and keep the meat warm.

10 In a saucepan over medium heat, combine the butter, morels, and ramps and cook for 5 minutes, then add the reduced duck stock. Taste for seasoning and add the peas. Keep warm.

11 Reheat the duck meat in a 400°F (205°C) oven for 10 minutes; slice the breast meat and cut the thighs in half. Add the thighs and legs to the morel sauce.

12 On a platter, lay down the breast slices and then cover the breastmeat with the peas, morels, and duck thighs and legs.

DUCK BREAST

radishes, bacon, and scallions

SERVES 4 TO 6

½ cup (125 g) minced bacon
4 duck breasts, trimmed and
  deboned
Sea salt and freshly ground
  black pepper
2 tablespoons (28 g) butter
2 cups (500 g) washed,
  trimmed, and quartered
  mixed-color radishes
1 bunch scallions, minced
2 shallots, sliced
1 tablespoon chopped fresh
  parsley

Here is a dish and a technique I know very well. In my five years at Michael's in Santa Monica, I grilled duck breast for hours on end. The mallard-Peking cross had a perfect skin, and they grilled well. The trick of the trade is to grill slowly on the skin side only. This will render the fat under the skin. Once the fat is rendered, the meat will cook for just a few more minutes to achieve a medium-rare breast.

1   Preheat the oven to 375°F (190°C).

2   In a cast-iron skillet, cook the bacon until golden, then remove the bacon from the pan and set aside; leave the bacon fat in the pan.

3   Season the duck breasts with salt and pepper and place them skin side down in the cast-iron skillet. Render the duck fat in the bacon fat until the skin turns brown. Cook the flesh side for 2 minutes, then remove breasts to a platter and let them sit.

4   Add the radishes to the pan and cook gently in the fat. Add the scallions and shallots and cook for 4 minutes. Discard the excess fat.

5   Return the bacon to the pan along with the remaining 2 tablespoons butter.

6   Cook the duck breasts in the oven for 10 minutes. Remove from the oven and cut lengthwise into long, delicate slices.

7   Garnish the duck pieces with the radish-scallion-bacon mixture and add the parsley. Serve warm.

CHICKEN RICHARD OLNEY

zucchini and herb stuffing

SERVES 8

1 pound (455 g) zucchini, shredded

2 teaspoons sea salt, plus more for seasoning the chicken

1 (3½-pound/1.6 kg) whole chicken

¾ cup (180 ml) ricotta

½ cup (50 g) grated Parmesan cheese

4 tablespoons (55 g) unsalted butter, softened

1 tablespoon chopped fresh oregano

1 egg yolk

2 tablespoons herbes de Provence

1 teaspoon freshly ground black pepper, plus more for seasoning the checking

2 tablespoons extra-virgin olive oil

This chicken recipe, which was a favorite in cookbook author Richard Olney's cooking classes, was originally published in his book *Simple French Food*. Spatchcocking, or removing the backbone and cooking the chicken flat, makes it cook more evenly and quickly. We recommend serving it with a powerful wine from Bandol or Barbera to show off its beauty and balance. For an easy dinner party experience, prep the chicken the night before and leave it uncovered on a rack in the refrigerator overnight.

1 Toss together the zucchini and 1 teaspoon of the salt. Leave to drain slightly in a sieve over a bowl. You want to remove the excess liquid but not squeeze the zucchini dry.

2 Place the chicken, breast side down, on a cutting board. Using poultry shears, cut along both sides of the backbone; remove and discard the backbone.

3 Turn the chicken breast side up. Place a heavy skillet on the chicken breast and press firmly against the breastbone until it cracks and the breast meat is an even 1 inch (2.5 cm) thick.

4 Cut off the wing tips.

5 Using your fingertips, gently loosen and lift the skin from the flesh of the breasts, thighs, and drumsticks, being careful not to tear or totally detach the skin. Set the prepped chicken aside.

6 Preheat the oven to 375°F (205°C).

7 Stir together the ricotta, Parmesan, butter, oregano, egg yolk, herbes de Provence, the zucchini mixture, the remaining 1 teaspoon salt, and 1 teaspoon of the pepper until combined.

8 Stuff the zucchini mixture under the skin of the chicken breast, thighs, and drumsticks. Mold and evenly distribute the stuffing, shaping and patting the skin on the outside of the chicken. Drizzle the oil over the chicken and season with salt and pepper.

9 Bake the chicken, basting every 15 minutes, until the skin is lightly browned and a meat thermometer inserted into the thickest portion of a thigh registers 165°F (71°C), about 1 hour. If the skin begins to get too dark, cover with aluminum foil.

10 Remove from the oven and let rest for 1 hour.

11 To serve, put the chicken back in the oven to reheat for 10 minutes, then carve into eight pieces and serve.

CARNE

A CONSCIOUS DECISION BY ME at the very outset of Barbuto was that the lesser cuts of pork, beef, and lamb would be a mainstay of the menu. This dictum has mostly rung true throughout the years, but on occasion I throw caution to the wind and toss in a New York steak, a whole spring lamb, or veal sweetbreads. The very nature of Barbuto is that it is a seasonal joint. And while meat is typically not viewed as a seasonal item, it does have a certain rhythm and pace.

Modern slaughterhouses have become more mechanized, and thus they neither slaughter under a full moon nor at the end of a heavy summer's bounty. These methods seem to have little or no place in our fast-paced world, but some producers appear to have their eyes on the past. They believe in a more naturalistic harvest of meat, one that celebrates their animals as treasures.

Barbuto is located in the former meat market of New York City. The connection to the meat market is a strong one, though sadly there are very few meat shops left in the immediate district. When I first lived on Horatio Street in the 1980s it was common to see whole carcasses of beef hanging by the awnings of the warehouses in the neighborhood. Now these buildings have either been razed or converted to chic restaurants, hotels, and retail shops. There are a few holdouts, and I suspect the old boys are not budging until they have to; money is not the object. These stalwart purveyors respect the old ways, and I for one long for the sight of whole lambs, pigs, and beef quarters waiting their turn to be cut up into chops and steaks.

A huge portion of the meat at Barbuto is cooked in our custom-designed oven built by Nobile Attie. All my chefs will back me when I say this cooking device is the heart and soul of Barbuto. It has saved our butts on many occasions; it is a robust and sleek box; it has cooked hundreds of thousands of JW Chickens and at least a hundred thousand steaks. Not bad for a bespoke device!

SKIRT STEAK ROMESCO

SERVES 6

Sea salt
2 pounds (910 g) trimmed
    skirt steak
Freshly ground black pepper
Olive oil
½ cup Romesco Salsa
    (page 250)
2 bunches spring onions,
    diced (about 2 cups)

This is a perennial favorite on the menu at Barbuto. It honors our philosophy of celebrating the lesser-known cuts and perhaps the better-value cuts as well. The skirt steak has become a very popular choice in today's market. I first happened upon skirt steak as a senior in high school. My buddy Tim and I had decided to camp out at Boot Jack Hill on Mount Tamalpais, a popular peak in Marin County, California. First we raided the local Safeway, where the cheapest cut by far was the skirt steak. It was wonderfully packaged in a tight pinwheel. We built fires and marinated the steak in cheap beer and then grilled them up. Served on San Francisco sourdough bread slathered in butter, the steak was a teenager's dream. At Barbuto romesco is our go-to dressing for skirt steak. It is an ancient Catalonian salsa that works wonders on many dishes.

1   Prepare an outdoor grill.

2   Cook the spring onions in boiling salted water for 5 minutes.

3   Season the steak with salt and pepper and then coat the meat with oil. Grill over a medium-hot fire until medium-rare, about 2 to 3 minutes on each side.

4   Slice the steak, slather with the romesco salsa, garnish with the onions, and serve.

PORK CHOPS AND MOSTARDA

SERVES 4

1 cup (220 g) brown sugar
½ cup (110 g) sea salt
2 tablespoons apple cider
    vinegar
4 bay leaves
4 (12-ounce/340 g) pork
    chops
3 tablespoons olive oil, divided
4 Jonagold apples, cored and
    cut in half
1 head mizuna or similar
    greens, washed and
    torn up
½ cup Mostarda (page 249)

Mostarda is a condiment that originates in the Emilia-Romagna. It was devised as a complement to heavy dishes like braised oxtail or *bollito misto*. It is fiery hot and spicy and has a lingering finish on the palate.

The pork chop here is brined in salt, brown sugar, and bay leaves. It creates a wonderful favor profile in the pork. The sweet-salty brine tenderizes the meat and then helps to create some good caramelization as you grill the chops over a fire.

1   In a 4-quart (4 L) pot, combine the brown sugar, salt, vinegar, bay leaves, and 1 quart (946 ml) water. Bring to a boil, reduce the heat to low, and cook for 1 hour. Let cool completely.

2   Add the pork chops to the brine. They can remain in the brine for a minimum of 12 hours or up to 3 days.

3   When ready to cook, remove the pork chops, pat dry, and coat with 2 tablespoons of the olive oil.

4   Prepare a charcoal or gas grill on medium heat.

5   Coat the apples with the remaining 1 tablespoon of olive oil and grill on the cut side for 5 minutes. Turn and grill another 5 to 10 minutes. They should be firm, not mushy.

6   Grill the chops 6 to 8 minutes per side for medium.

7   Toss the greens with ¼ teaspoon fine sea salt and a drizzle of oilve oil.

8   Mix the apples and mostarda; serve the chops with this mixture and sprinkle with greens.

LAMB CHOPS WITH MINT BUTTER

MAKES 8 CHOPS

American-raised lamb chops are a wonder. These days lamb consumption is on the wane, sadly. I imagine that back in the day, sheep were a valuable commodity. They were a triple threat, providing wool, grazing to help claim pasture, and of course meat. One hundred years ago, Americans ate three times the amount of lamb that we eat today. I think in part we have lost a taste for the meat, and we regard it as gamey. This is to some extent the fault of the butchers, who slaughter lambs that are not technically (by European standards) spring lamb but closer to mutton. The larger chops that steakhouses use can be quite strong in flavor and may be the source of the gamey-lamb complaint.

The market has been inundated lately with New Zealand and Australian lamb. These are much smaller, perhaps more like spring lamb, and they can be better-tasting than the domestic variety. The product is likely to be frozen, and though I am not generally a fan of frozen meat, the Australian variety in particular is quite good. Shoulder meat is tougher but more flavorful. The technique for preparing the chops is quite straightforward and the cooking is not elaborate, but the results are spectacular. *recipe continues*

206

1 (2-pound) rack of lamb, cut
    into 8 chops*
Sea salt and freshly ground
    black pepper
2 tablespoons olive oil
2 tablespoons butter
¼ cup (60 ml) fresh mint

* *Many supermarkets have these
    ready to go, or you can ask
    your butcher to prepare them
    for you.*

1   Season the chops well with salt and pepper.

2   In a heavy cast-iron skillet, heat the olive oil over medium heat. Add 1 tablespoon of the butter, and when foaming, add the chops, flat side down.

3   Cook until the chops are brown and crispy, about 8 minutes, then turn over and brown the other side. Place the chops on a warm platter.

4   Add 1 tablespoon cold water to the skillet. Reheat the pan and add the remaining 1 tablespoon butter and the mint. Whisk together, and then drizzle the sauce over the chops.

HANGER STEAK WITH SALSA PICANTE

SERVES 4

1½ pounds (910 g) hanger
    steak, cut into 2 steaks
Sea salt and freshly ground
    black pepper
1 tablespoon red wine
2 tablespoons olive oil
Salsa Picante (page 250)

Hanger is a funny cut of meat. It has taken me a long time to make friends with it. The trick is to cut it on the thick side and not overcook it, while ensuring it is well crisped on the exterior. This steak vies with the skirt as the most popular at Barbuto. It is very meaty and has a delicious iron-like quality. It is neither tough nor tender, a real meat lover's steak. The hanger does have to be trimmed carefully, as it has sinews and gristle that need to be removed. It is still relatively reasonably priced; however, the market has changed, and the cost of meat is on the rise. The hanger is a good steak to marinate or not. It loves a good amount of sea salt and pepper and, as in this recipe, it is well paired with salsa picante.

1   Prepare a grill to medium heat.

2   Season the steaks with salt and pepper. Sprinkle each steak with the wine and 1 tablespoon of the oil.

3   Dry off the steaks and then grill for about 8 minutes per side, or to desired doneness. Let rest to reabsorb and distribute the juices.

4   Slice the steaks and serve with the salsa.

PORK CHOP MILANESE AL OUVO

wilted swiss chard, bacon & cream

SERVES 4

2 bunches small rainbow
    chard
8 tablespoons (120 ml) olive
    oil
4 tablespoons minced bacon,
    about two rashers
1 small onion, diced
3 cloves garlic, sliced
Sea salt
¼ cup (60 ml) plus 1
    tablespoon heavy cream
10 tablespoons (140 g) butter
4 (10-ounce/280 g) pork
    chops with rib bone
    attached (make sure they
    aren't too fatty, as some
    heritage breeds can be)
6 eggs
1 cup (125 g) all-purpose flour
Freshly ground black pepper
1–2 cups (70–140 g) fresh
    breadcrumbs
1 tablespoon capers
8 anchovy fillets
Juice of 1 lemon

This is a decadent dish, worthy of a very special occasion. The gratin of Swiss chard and bacon is almost a meal unto itself, and the pork is something you will never forget. It is true mountain food, great after a long hike or skiing the cold slopes of the Dolomites.

The salty anchovies and capers are a scrumptious umami addition to the crunchy breadcrumb exterior of the Milanese. You can also use veal chops here; this would make it a more authentic and classic dish.

1   Trim the chard. Mince all the chard including the stems. Wash thoroughly.

2   In a heavy pot, heat 6 tablespoons (90 ml) of the oil over medium heat; add the bacon, onion, and garlic. Cook until the onion and garlic are tender, then add salt.

3   Add the chard and cook quickly, then add ¼ cup (60 ml) cream. When the chard is tender, add 4 tablespoons (55 g) of the butter and stir well.

4   With a pounding tool, whack the pork chops so you achieve uniform thickness of about ⅓ inch (8 mm).

5   Mix 2 of the eggs with the remaining 1 tablespoon cream and season with salt.

6   Season the flour with salt and pepper.

7   Dredge the chops in the flour, then the egg mixture. Leave the chops in the egg mixture for 10 minutes.

8   One at a time, remove them and dredge in the bread-crumbs. Lay on a counter topped with parchment paper.

9   Heat a 10-inch (25 cm) cast-iron skillet over medium-high heat. Add 1 tablespoon oil and 2 tablespoons butter to the pan and heat until golden.

10   Slide 2 of the chops into the pan and cook until golden on each side, about 4 minutes per side. Set aside and repeat with the remaining chops, replenishing the butter and oil as needed.

11   Add 1 tablespoon butter and 1 tablespoon oil to the pan, break the remaining 4 eggs into the pan, and fry the eggs sunny side up. Place 1 egg on each chop.

12   Add the capers and anchovies to the pan, cook for 2 minutes, and place on top of the eggs. Deglaze the pan with the lemon juice and drizzle it over the capers and anchovies. Serve with the chard.

ST. JOHN LAMB

2 (5-pound) lamb shoulders
Sea salt and freshly ground
    black pepper
4 onions, peeled
2 heads garlic, peeled
4 large carrots, peeled and
    chopped
1 (750 ml) bottle cheap white
    wine
8 sprigs fresh rosemary, plus
    1 tablespoon chopped
    fresh rosemary leaves
1 bay leaf
3 tablespoons (45 ml) olive oil
4 leeks, sliced and washed
    thoroughly
2 tablespoons (55 g) butter

Fergus Henderson and his wife, Margot, are perhaps the happiest and most generous chefs I know. We bonded in Australia, where we spent a week cooking at a casino in Melbourne. His team from St. John in London, perhaps the quintessential English farm-to-table restaurant, came to cook a luncheon to launch Fergus's latest book. My crew was just mesmerized. Fergus wanted to do some lamb shoulders. His team blast-roasted them whole in the oven until they were cooked through and then served them with salsa verde. Here is my version.

1   Preheat the oven to 375°F (190°C).

2   Season the lamb shoulders with sea salt and pepper, place them in a heavy roasting pan, and add 2 cups (480 ml) water. Roast for 2 hours.

3   Add the onions, garlic, and carrots to the pan. Roast for another 45 minutes or until the lamb is tender and nicely browned.

4   Remove the meat and vegetables and let cool.

5   When the lamb is cool enough to touch, pick the meat off the bones (save the bones). Shred the meat so it will be easy to eat. Mix with the cooked onions, carrots, and garlic. Place the meat and vegetables in the refrigerator.

6   Deglaze the roasting pan with the wine. Put the bones back in the pan. Add 1 quart cold water, bring to a boil, and then simmer on the stovetop for 1 hour.

7   Strain through a mesh strainer and keep warm on the stovetop. Discard the bones.

8   Cook the leeks in a saucepan in simmering salted water. When cooked to tender, remove. Discard the water.

9   Remove lamb and onion mixture from the refrigerator and add to a 6-quart stock pot.

10   Add the lamb stock and leeks and reheat for 10 minutes

11   Add 1 tablespoon chopped rosemary leaves and 2 table-spoons butter. Season with sea salt and pepper.

12   Serve hot in soup bowls.

LEG OF LAMB

SERVES 10 AS
AN ENTRÉE

1 boneless leg of lamb
Sea salt and freshly ground
    black pepper
¼ cup (60 ml) extra-virgin
    olive oil
3 tablespoons chopped fresh
    rosemary leaves
2 tablespoons chopped fresh
    sage
½ teaspoon red chile flakes
6 anchovy fillets, finely
    chopped
6 cloves garlic, finely chopped
Zest of 1 lemon
1 cup (240 ml) red wine
Salsa Verde (page 250)

A good party dish. This is a fun take on the proverbial por-chetta recipe, perfect for those who either eschew pork or prefer lamb. Lamb is rich meat that takes well to roasting in this fashion. At Barbuto we can place a dish like this in the center of the kitchen table, and then the folks can grab the dish and serve themselves. It really makes it a party!

1   Preheat the oven to 450°F (230°C).

2   Arrange the lamb on a work surface and butterfly any larger muscles so the lamb is flattened to an even thickness. Season assertively on both sides with salt and pepper.

3   In a small bowl, mix together the oil, rosemary, sage, chile flakes, anchovies, garlic, and lemon zest to make a paste. Rub the lamb all over with the paste.

4   Roll the lamb like a jelly roll and tie in 1-inch (2.5 cm) intervals with butcher's twine.

5   Arrange the lamb on a rack set inside a rimmed bak-ing sheet. Pour 1 cup (240 ml) water and the wine into the baking sheet. Roast the lamb, turning once, until lightly browned, about 25 minutes.

6   Reduce the oven temperature to 350°F (175°C) and continue to roast, turning once, until an instant-read ther-mometer inserted in the thickest part of lamb reads 135°F (57°C), about 50 minutes.

7   Let the lamb rest on a carving board for 15 minutes. (Meanwhile, make the salsa verde.) Remove the twine, slice the lamb, and serve with salsa verde.

PORCHETTA

**SERVES 14
GENEROUSLY**

½ cup fresh sage leaves, finely chopped

¼ cup fresh rosemary leaves, finely chopped

¼ cup fresh oregano leaves, finely chopped

12 cloves garlic, peeled and blanched for 5 minutes in salted simmering water

3 tablespoons (20 g) fennel pollen (availalble from online retailers; alternately, you can use fennel seeds)

3 tablespoons grated lemon zest

1 (2-pound/905 g) pork belly, skin on

1 (5-pound/2.3 kg) pork loin

Sea salt and freshly ground black pepper

Justin Smillie, the effervescent chef at Upland, was at Barbuto for a few years. He definitely left his mark on the restaurant. His large frame and ever-so-large personality helped push Barbuto forward. He loved to explore the boundaries of Italian cookery and he was infatuated with porchetta. At first I was skeptical, but his efforts to make a wonderful porchetta proved out. Here is my interpretation of Justin's dish. The meat cures in salt and pepper in the fridge for three days, so plan a little ahead for this special meal.

1   In a medium bowl, mix together the sage, rosemary, oregano, garlic, fennel pollen, and lemon zest; set aside.

2   Place the pork belly skin side up on a clean work surface. Using a very sharp knife, score the skin in a diamond-shape pattern. Turn the pork belly over so that it is skin side down.

3   Place the pork loin on a cutting board. Holding the blade of the knife parallel to the board, cut along the length of the pork loin, but not all the way through.

4   Unfold so that it opens like a book. Place the butterflied loin on top of the pork belly.

5   Spread the herb mixture over the pork loin and season with salt and pepper. Roll the pork away from you into a cylindrical shape so the pork belly encases the pork loin; tie with butcher's twine at 1-inch (2.5 cm) intervals to make snug.

6   Season the pork belly skin with salt and pepper. Place in the refrigerator, uncovered, to air-dry for 3 days.

7   Fit a rimmed baking sheet with a rack and transfer the pork to the rack; let stand until the pork comes to room temperature, about 2 hours.

8   Preheat the oven to 500°F (260°C) with a rack set in the lower third of the oven.

9   Transfer the pork to the oven and cook until the skin begins to crackle, about 10 minutes.

10   Lower the oven temperature to 325°F (165°C) and continue roasting until an instant-read thermometer inserted into the center of the roast reaches 130°F (54°C), about 3 hours. Let stand for 30 minutes before slicing and serving.

PORK STEW

roasted hatch chiles

½ cup (120 ml) olive oil

2 pounds (910 g) pork
shoulder, trimmed and
diced

Sea salt and freshly ground
black pepper

1 onion, diced

2 leeks, washed and diced

2 bulbs fennel, cored and
diced

6 shallots, diced

3 cloves garlic, sliced

1 (750 ml) bottle Sauvignon
Blanc

2 cups (300 g) diced fresh
Hatch chiles, stemmed,
seeded, and diced
(poblano chiles can be
substituted)

2 tablespoons julienned fresh
sage

Here is an ode to my first trips to France and Italy. So many fancy places either ignored pork or cooked it poorly. I relished dining at the lowly country tavern, where pork was a long, slow-cooked affair, festooned with the flavors and odors of garlic, onions, and fennel. In this fashion pork meat becomes elevated—succulent and tender.

1   In a large heavy casserole, heat ¼ cup (60 ml) of the oil over medium-high heat. Season the pieces of pork with salt and pepper and sear them hard in the oil. By this I mean to really crisp and brown the meat.

2   Remove the pork and add 2 tablespoons of the oil to the casserole. Add the onion, leeks, fennel, and shallots. Sauté until golden, then add the garlic.

3   Return the pork to the casserole and then add the wine and 2 cups (480 ml) cold water.

4   Bring to a boil, then immediately reduce the heat to a simmer. Cover and cook for about 2 hours, until the pork is fork tender. Stir every 30 minutes.

5   Preheat the oven to 400°F (205°C).

6   Cook the chiles in a sauté pan with the remaining 2 tablespoons oil and sea salt to taste. Roast in the oven for 15 minutes.

7   Add the roasted chiles to the pork casserole about 30 minutes before the stew is done. When the stew is cooked, season again with salt and pepper, add the sage, and serve.

RIB-EYE STEAK

grilled lemon and grilled spigarello

SERVES 4

1 large bowl mixed hardy
greens (such as kale and
spigarello)
2 tablespoons olive oil, plus
more for drizzling
Sea salt
2 (12-ounce/340 g) boneless
rib-eye steaks
Freshly ground black pepper
4 lemons (trim ends and cut
each into three rounds)
2 cloves garlic, peeled and
smashed

This is an elegant meal that I love to make for special occasions. My friend Paul Kahan, a highly accomplished chef from Chicago, and I do a lot of charity work, and one of our favorites benefits the very noble cause of fighting childhood leukemia; it's called Alex's Lemonade. We were asked to do a special dinner at one of Paul's restaurants, Big Star. He knows how much I love rib-eye steak, so that's where we started. He picked some kale and spigarella from his backyard garden, produced some beautiful aged steaks, and let me have some fun.

1   In a large bowl, toss the greens with the oil and season with salt.

2   Prepare a grill.

3   Season the steaks with sea salt and freshly ground pepper and grill them until rare (the rule of thumb is 8 minutes per side). Let rest.

4   At the same time, grill the lemon slices until quite tender and brown on both sides. Set the steaks and lemons aside.

5   Clean the grill grate well with a grill brush. When it's clean, dump the greens on top of the grill, let them cook for a few minutes, and, with your long kitchen tongs, gently turn them over. Repeat until they are wilted and cooked. Return the greens to the bowl and toss with the lemons and garlic.

6   Place the steaks back on the grill to come up to the desired temperature. Place the greens and lemons on a platter, slice the meat, and decorate the greens with the slices.

7   Drizzle some oil on top and then sprinkle with a bit of pepper and salt and serve.

VENISON WITH BRAISED CARDOONS

4 (5-ounce/140 g) venison
   steaks, trimmed of
   silverskin and fat
Freshly ground black pepper
1 onion, sliced
3 carrots, washed and sliced
3 cloves garlic, smashed
1 cup (240 ml) red wine
2 bay leaves
1 cup (200 g) fresh parsley
   stems
1 pound (455 g) cardoons,
   washed and trimmed
1 teaspoon all-purpose flour
Sea salt
4 shallots, peeled and minced
2 leeks, washed, trimmed, and
   julienned
9 tablespoons (140 g) butter
1 cup (240 ml) chicken stock
3 tablespoons grated
   Parmesan cheese
2 tablespoons chopped fresh
   chives

I fell in love with game when I worked in France after attending cooking school in Paris. I loved it all: wild boar, venison, wild ducks, and so on. The way chefs approached venison in those days was very old school. The meat would get a game marinade of onions, garlic, carrots, vinegar, and wine. Sometimes we would leave them in the marinade for a week if they were older. The venison we get in the U.S. is less gamey and therefore needs far less time in a marinade. You also want to preserve the intrinsic flavor profile of the venison rather than mask the beautiful taste that comes about when you sauté it.

Cardoons are magical beasts. They are the weirdest vegetables out there, and perhaps the least understood. They have a bitter, artichoke-like quality. They do require two cooking methods: they need to first be poached in a white liquid and then cooked again in chicken stock.

1   Season the steaks with pepper.

2   Make the marinade: In a nonreactive roasting pan combine the onion, carrots, garlic, wine, bay leaves, and parsley stems. Mix well, add the venison steaks, and marinate overnight.

3 Slice the cardoons and cook them in simmering water with the flour (this is an old French technique called "cuire a blanc" that is meant keep them from oxidizing) and 1 teaspoon salt. Cook for about 30 minutes, until tender, then drain.

4 Preheat the oven to 350?°F (175°C).

5 In a sauté pan, cook the shallots and leeks in 2 tablespoons of the butter over low heat for 5 minutes. Season with salt and pepper.

6 Rub an enameled baking dish with 1 tablespoon butter and add the cardoons, stock, an additional 2 tablespoons butter, the shallots, and leeks.

7 Bake for 30 minutes, until golden.

8 Preheat the broiler. Sprinkle the cardoons with the cheese and place under the broiler until golden brown.

9 Remove the venison steaks from the marinade, reserving the marinade. Dry the steaks and season well with salt and pepper.

10 In a cast-iron skillet, heat 2 tablespoons of the butter over medium heat.

11 Cook the steaks in the butter for about 8 minutes on each side or until medium-rare. Remove the steaks to a serving plate and strain the liquid from the marinade into the pan. Cook until reduced to ½ cup. Add the remaining 2 tablespoons butter and the chives.

12 Season and sauce the venison steaks. Serve with the cardoons.

HANGER STEAK AND ARUGULA

SERVES 4

1 (18-ounce/510 g) hanger
   steak, trimmed of fat and
   sinew
Sea salt and cracked black
   pepper
2 tablespoons olive oil
10 ounces (285 g) baby
   arugula
3 tablespoons grated
   Parmesan cheese
1 tablespoon balsamic vinegar

This is pure Barbuto! I think we concocted this as a lunch item very early on. It has remained on the daytime menu since. When devising the original menu for Barbuto, I really aimed for recipes that were dead simple yet filled with flavor and nuance. Dishes that captured the essence of the ingredients, that harmonize with a simple "do re me." And here you have that essence, a grilled hanger steak, some garden-fresh arugula, grated Parmesan. Add sea salt, olive oil, and a few turns of black pepper, and voilà, a perfect luncheon salad.

1   Season the steak with sea salt and pepper.

2   Heat 1 tablespoon of the oil in a cast-iron skillet large enough to hold the hanger steak, over medium-high heat. Sear the steak until crispy on all sides.

3   Cover the skillet and lower heat to medium, Total cook time for medium-rare should be 8 to 10 minutes.

4   Place the arugula in a large bowl. Add the cheese, vinegar, and olive oil.

5   Slice the steak as thinly as possible. Add to the bowl and toss. Season with salt and pepper.

CONTORNI ~
VEGETABLES

THERE WAS A VERY DELIBERATE effort at the beginning of Barbuto not to follow the norms of a standard Italian restaurant. For instance, it was an imperative for us not to crowd the plate; we felt that it was okay to serve a beautifully cooked fish with a spoonful of sauce and that was it. If anyone felt they needed to have more food, they could by all means order from the Contorni menu. And we established this philosophy for all main courses. In this vegetable chapter, I really get to spread my wings.

Vegetables are my secret passion. I love, revere, and worship them. However, this wasn't always the case; as a kid I could not stand the sight or the taste of any vegetable. I can't remember my turning point, but somewhere along the line, thankfully, it happened.

I am at home rummaging around in a vegetable garden. Nothing is more satisfying than to harvest warm spuds, delicate squash blossoms, string beans, cauliflower, and all the rest. The feel of dirt on freshly dug-up leeks, the majesty of the artichoke, and the awkward look of a Brussels sprout stalk.

If you can, start a little garden, even an herb garden on your windowsill. The pleasures of seeding new crops, or the preparation of last season's potatoes to start a new season, are a revelation. My cooks in the kitchen at Barbuto get this; they understand that the flavors of freshly picked, organic vegetables on the table are without parallel. Not all of us have the luxury, but please try to visit a farm soon. Supporting our farmers is crucial, and you will feel better about everything.

I would like to see you try a myriad of new vegetables, from the ubiquitous (zucchini) to the slightly esoteric (sunchokes) to the really unusual (cardoons and rutabaga).

MASHED POTATOES

2 pounds (910 g) Yukon Gold
potatoes
6 cloves garlic, peeled and left
whole
Sea salt
2 tablespoons (60 ml) olive oil
½ cup (240 ml) heavy cream
¼ cup (½ stick/115 g) butter

A perennial favorite at the Waxman house! This recipe explores the most decadent treatment of potatoes: the garlic adds depth, the olive oil adds fruitiness and finesse, and the cream makes it luxurious. And the butter doesn't hinder anything at all. The tip here is to find potatoes that are pristine, blemish free. The second tip is to reserve the cooking liquid to create a creamy and smooth texture and add depth.

1   Wash and trim the potatoes. Cut them into 2-inch (5 cm) blocks.

2   Put the potatoes and garlic in a pot and cover with cold water. Bring to a boil, then add 1 teaspoon salt. Reduce the heat to a murmur. Simmer slowly until the potatoes are tender, about 30 minutes. Pour off all but ½ cup (120 ml) of the cooking liquid. Return the potatoes to the heat and add the oil and cream.

3   Using an immersion blender or an old-fashioned potato masher if you don't have an immersion blender, gently puree the potatoes, cream, oil, and garlic over the heat.

4   Add the butter and continue to puree, then taste for seasoning. Serve hot.

PAN-ROASTED VEGETABLES

**SERVES 4
AS A SIDE DISH**

Sea salt
1 rutabaga, peeled and cut
    into chunks
2 parsnips, peeled and cut into
    chunks
1 celery root, peeled and cut
    into chunks
2 Yukon Gold potatoes,
    washed and cut into
    chunks
4 turnips, washed and cut into
    chunks
3 leeks
6 tablespoons (85 g) butter
4 tablespoons olive oil

Here is a chance to establish a great accompanist to any main course. These roasted vegetables are versatile, and the technique is a good one to master. The seasonal component is the most important factor; at Barbuto, we love scouring the farmer's market for the best turnips, carrots, pumpkin, potatoes, and fennel. The season will dictate what makes the most sense and help you understand what combination of vegetables will work together.

In autumn, you might have Brussels sprouts, cauliflower, romanesco, and artichokes; in spring, carrots, small turnips, fingerling potatoes, and spring onions; and in winter, rutabaga, parsnips, cabbage. The rule of thumb is to experiment a bit, finding what combination works well. I have given you a template. The standard procedure is to cook hard vegetables (rutabaga, potatoes, etc.) in simmering salted water before roasting. More tender vegetables (fennel, tomatoes, zucchini) can be added without pre-cooking.

1   Prepare a pot of simmering salted water. Cook all the vegetables in the water in two batches: The rutabaga, parsnips, and celery root will cook together. This will take about 35 minutes.

2   Repeat above but with the potatoes, turnips, and leeks. This will take about 25 minutes. When all the vegetables are cooked, heat a large Dutch oven over medium heat. Add the butter and oil. Cook all the vegetables together until golden and tender, about 5 to 7 minutes, stirring occasionally. Season with salt and serve with a main dish.

SAUTÉED GREENS

garlic and pecorino

SERVES 4

2 tablespoons olive oil
1 large onion, sliced
4 cloves garlic, smashed
Sea salt
2 cups each roughly chopped
    spinach, kale, and chard
4 tablespoons (55 g) butter
2 tablespoons heavy cream
    (optional)
2 tablespoons grated Pecorino
    Romano cheese

This wonderful dish is a mainstay—a go-to on the menu at Barbuto. The greens should be seasonal, and this recipe makes grand use of leftover or soon-to-be-discarded bruised outer leaves of lettuce and cabbage. The formula is fairly set in stone: two cloves of garlic, smashed and slightly cooked in olive oil, a mix of greens, and the most important ingredient—water. As most greens are 90 percent water, one would think that they needed no extra water to extract their intrinsic powers. Not true. The water acts as a cushion, preventing the greens from becoming too dry or, worse, flavorless.

1   In a heatproof casserole, heat the oil, onion, garlic, and some salt. Cook over medium-high heat for 3 minutes, stirring constantly.

2   Add the greens and stir well. Add the butter, cream (if using), and ⅔ cup water.

3   Cover and cook until the greens are just wilted.

4   Season with salt, garnish with the cheese, and serve.

SUNCHOKES WITH PAPRIKA AIOLI

SERVES 4 TO 6

1 pound (455 g) sunchokes, washed and diced
2 tablespoons butter
½ teaspoon each sea salt and freshly ground black pepper
1 tablespoon paprika
1 cup (240 ml) Aioli (page 249)

I love sunchokes. They have superb, nutty flavor and a sinuous, silky texture. I used to peel them, but lately I just wash them thoroughly and then either cook them whole or cut them into interesting shapes. Sunchokes are hard to mess up. The worst-case scenario is to turn them into a puree if all else fails! They are very versatile, they pair well with many other vegetables, meats, and poultry. They are incredibly nutritious and unusual; lots of folks prefer them to potatoes, including me!

1   Preheat the oven to 400°F (205°C).

2   In a roasting pan, combine ½ cup (120 ml) water, the sunchokes, and butter. Season with the salt and pepper; then roast for 35 minutes, or until golden and tender.

3   Stir the paprika into the aioli.

4   Serve the sunchokes warm with the aioli on the side.

WILTED CHARD AND HAZELNUTS

SERVES 4

2 heads of rainbow chard
3 cloves garlic, peeled and
 thinly sliced
2 tablespoons olive oil
Sea salt
4 tablespoons (55 g) butter
2 tablespoons roasted
 hazelnuts, crushed

I had no idea how much of a love affair I would embark upon when I first encountered Swiss chard. I thought it looked unappetizing raw, and I never gave it a second look until much later in my career. I never ordered it in a restaurant and avoided it when I saw it in the market. Its charms eluded me. The big "a-ha" moment came in Switzerland, at a mountain resort in Verbier. I had a dish of venison, and the side dish was Swiss chard in a casserole, hot and bubbly with Gruyère spilling over the edge. The first incendiary bite was a total shock: *Where have you been?* I asked. The earthy, dense texture and quite unexpected umami quality threw me. The vegetable has become a standby at Barbuto. I have no idea why folks discard the stems, but they are essential to the flavor of the dish.

1   Wash and mince the rainbow chard, stems and all.

2   In a large saucepan, cook the garlic and olive oil for 2 minutes over medium heat, then add the rainbow chard. Season with salt. Add 2 tablespoons butter and ½ cup (120 ml) cold water.

3   Cook the chard until the leaves are tender and cooked through, about 5 minutes. Take care not to overcook.

4   Add the hazelnuts and the remaining 2 tablespoons butter and cook for 5 minutes. Serve hot.

SUCCOTASH

SERVES 6
AS A SIDE DISH

2 tablespoons olive oil
3 tablespoons butter
1 sweet onion, diced
2 poblano chiles, diced
2 zucchini, diced
Sea salt
2 ears of corn
½ cup (65 g) edamame
    (boiled for 6 minutes in
    salted water)
½ cup (65 g) cranberry beans
    (boiled for 6 minutes in
    salted water)
½ cup (55 g) topped and
    diced string beans
2 heirloom tomatoes
1 tablespoon each minced
    basil, chives, parsley, and
    mint
Freshly ground black pepper

Two years ago, at the U.S. Open of tennis, I was invited to do a demonstration cooking class with the wonderful Venus Williams. I love doing demonstrations, and I was really looking forward to doing this with Venus. Her management told me she was pretty easygoing and it would not take a lot of effort to get her to help me cook onstage. The only caveat was that Venus was vegan. That made sense: a top-flight athlete adhering to a strict diet, seeing the practical and logical training methodology. So, wishing to make her happy, I devised a recipe I thought she would appreciate. We performed onstage at the W Hotel in Midtown Manhattan.

Venus is a tall, incredibly beautiful, and slightly daunting personality. I decided to plunge in and just get her to help me cook. I have to say, it was the most fun I have had in a demonstration. Not only was Venus cooperative and funny, but she really wanted to cook.

Succotash is a pretty straightforward recipe. The word "succotash" comes from early Native Americans, who evidently were quite fond of fresh beans at the summer's end. This version has corn, peppers, three types of beans, onions, fresh herbs, and butter. Since I knew that Venus was vegan, I planned to omit the butter. I asked Venus what her favorite ingredient in the recipe was, and she replied, "Butter"! So I had a good laugh with her and asked how much butter she wanted to use, and she replied, "Loads!" So here you have my succotash for Venus Williams.

1   In a casserole, heat the oil and 1 tablespoon of the butter over medium-high heat and cook the onion, poblanos, and zucchini with salt for about 5 minutes.

2   Cut the corn kernels off the cobs and add them to the casserole. Continue cooking for another 8 to 10 minutes.

3   Cook the edamame, cranberry beans, and string beans in boiling water until tender; drain and add to the casserole.

4   Dice the tomatoes and add them to the casserole. Add the remaining 2 tablespoons butter and the herbs and season with salt and pepper.

5   Serve hot or at room temperature.

ROASTED BEETS

fresh farmer's cheese and pistachio

SERVES 8

Sea salt
2 pounds (910 g) medium-
    sized beets with tops
    removed
2 tablespoons butter
2 tablespoons pistachio oil
2 tablespoons fresh farmer's
    cheese (we like to use
    Cloumage, from Shy
    Brothers Farm; you could
    also substitute fresh
    ricotta)
2 tablespoons pistachios,
    toasted
Freshly ground black pepper
Upland cress, for garnish

Beets have become the catchword for healthy veg. And indeed, they truly are. What is more interesting is the discovery of heirloom varieties. These ancient cultivars are so essential to my cooking that I sometimes take them for granted. Yellow beets, Chioggia beets, black sand beets—they all have their different qualities. Some are better small, others need to reach a good size before the sugars are set and the starchiness has dissipated.

Over the years I've tried various cooking methods: wrapped in tinfoil on fireplace coals, on a bed of salt in a slow oven, poached in salted water, sautéed in a ceramic pan, and roasted in a closed container. All these work wonders, but steaming in a pressure cooker might be the best. Here we simmer on the stovetop, cool, peel, and then roast in the oven. It is best to use surgical gloves when peeling beets to avoid staining your fingers.

1   In a pot, bring 2 quarts (2 liters) water to a boil, add some salt and the beets, cover, reduce the heat to a simmer, and cook for 30 minutes or until the beets are tender.

2   Let the beets cool in the cooking liquid, then drain. Peel and dice them.

3   Preheat the oven to 375°F (190°C).

4   Put the beets, butter, and pistachio oil in a roasting pan. Season with sea salt and pepper; cook for 30 minutes.

5   Place the farmer's cheese in a serving bowl, add the cooked beets and the toasted pistachios, and sprinkle with sea salt and freshly ground black pepper. Garnish with upland cress. Serve at room temperature.

CAULIFLOWER SOUFFLÉ

SERVES 4 AS A
SIDE DISH

1 head cauliflower
2 tablespoons Roquefort
   cheese
4 tablespoons (55 g) butter
½ cup (120 ml) heavy cream
1 tablespoon chopped fresh
   chives

This recipe is a love affair between two seemingly polar opposites—Roquefort, the mighty blue from southwest France, and cauliflower, a hearty vegetable that is a bit shy of flavor and needs coaxing to extract its intrinsic goodness. The two marry in an extraordinary fashion. This dish, while called a soufflé, is really more of a puffy casserole; the soufflé notion is a tribute to the fast cook time and high heat.

1   Preheat the oven to 400°F (205°C).

2   Put water in a saucepot, top with a steamer basket, and bring the water to a simmer. Place the whole head of cauliflower in the basket, cover, and cook for 20 minutes, or until tender.

3   Mix the cheese with 2 tablespoons of the butter and the cream.

4   Remove the cauliflower from the steamer and place the whole head in a buttered 4-quart soufflé mold. Top the cauliflower with the cream and the cheese butter. Bake for 20 minutes. Sprinkle with the chives and serve.

ROASTED ROMANESCO

SERVES 6

2 heads whole romanesco
Sea salt
½ cup (115 g) butter, plus
    more for the casserole
    dish
4 tablespoons grated Gruyère
    cheese
2 tablespoons butter

If you wander through the galleries of the Louvre or the Uffizi or the Met in New York and study still-life paintings of food, you will be amazed at how inviting the vegetables of the Old Masters appear. They look more vibrant, richer, and more delicious (at least to the eye) than our present-day vegetables. One that has made a huge resurgence lately is the romanesco. It is a superb vegetable and a geometric marvel. It dazzles any diner and, if really fresh, tastes fantastic. It's relatively simple to cook, though one has to remember not to overcook it; it can become very cabbage-y if cooked too long in butter or oil. It looks like something out of an Escher painting, an endless sequence of ever-expanding spirals.

1   Preheat the oven to 400°F (205°C).

2   Slice the florets off the romanesco. Cut them in half lengthwise.

3   Bring a large pot of salted water to a boil.

4   Add the romanesco florets and cook for 8 minutes, until tender. Drain.

5   In a bowl, toss together the romanesco, butter, and cheese.

6   Butter a casserole dish and add the romanesco. Season well with sea salt.

7   Bake for 30 minutes, or until golden and cooked through. Serve hot.

BARBUTO POTATOES

**SERVES 4 TO 6
AS A SIDE DISH**

Sea salt
1 head garlic, cut in half along
the equator
4 sprigs fresh rosemary
4 russet potatoes (about 2½
pounds / 48 ounces)
1 cup (285 ml) canola oil
¼ cup (25 g) grated Pecorino
Romano cheese
Fine sea salt

One of my customers asked me if we added crack to these potatoes—he found them addictive. So do many other folks. To be truthful, there is really nothing special about them; they are just good organic russets, cooked gently with garlic and rosemary and fried. Then they're tossed with pecorino, which adds umami, salt, and fried rosemary leaves. That is it. In any case, if you find them addictive, I warned you!

1   Fill a large stockpot with water and add 1 tablespoon salt, the halved head of garlic, and 2 sprigs rosemary.

2   Add the potatoes, bring to a boil, and then lower heat to simmer. Cook until the potatoes are tender, about 40 to 50 minutes. You want them just cooked through, not soft.

3   Let cool in the cooking liquid. Remove the potatoes and discard cooking liquid.

4   Put a 10-inch (25 cm) cast-iron pan on the stovetop, add the oil, and heat the oil to 300°F (150°C).

5   Crush each potato gently with your hand and add half the potatoes to the skillet.

6   Cook the potatoes for 10 to 20 minutes or until deep golden brown. Remove the potatoes with tongs and drain the potatoes in a bowl lined with paper towels. Repeat with the remaining potatoes and the remaining rosemary.

7   Remove the paper towel, add the cheese and some salt, and toss well. Serve hot.

BRUSSELS SPROUTS BARBUTO

**SERVES 4
AS A SIDE DISH**

2½ tablespoons (60 ml) olive oil
4 cups (350–400 g) Brussels sprouts, trimmed and cut in half
Sea salt
2 small or medium cloves garlic, in their skins
Freshly cracked black pepper
2 tablespoons (55 g) butter
3 tablespoons hazelnuts or walnuts, roasted and skinned

I apologize for the amount of Brussels sprouts in this book. They are just so yummy! From raw to fried to roasted, they are incredibly versatile and so good for you. Here is a perfect way to cook them. We make these to order at Barbuto, so I can vouch that this is a speedy recipe. We split the medium-sized Brussels sprouts in half and sauté them at a ferocious tempo over high heat. At home, we will achieve the same effect, but cooking a bit differently. We take the cut side, oil it and season it, place it on the surface of the pan, and then gradually bring the temperature up. Once we hear the right sound, we know the Brussels are cooking well. This will ensure a crisp, golden brown caramelization, the same effect you'd get if you were cooking at Barbuto in the heat of battle!

1   Heat the olive oil in a cast-iron pan over medium heat.

2   Add the Brussels sprouts, cut side down, and season with sea salt. Add the garlic.

3   Cook for about 20 minutes, gently tossing the contents as you go, until the sprouts are golden and sizzling in the pan. Add some freshly cracked black pepper. Remove the garlic cloves from the pan. Remove the skins and cut the cloves in half.

4   Return the garlic to the pan and add the butter. Season with sea salt and add the hazelnuts.

5   Toss well and serve hot.

ROASTED TURNIPS

anchovy butter

**SERVES 4 TO 6
AS A SIDE DISH**

2 bunches turnips with greens,
     cut in half
4 tablespoons (55 g) butter
1 clove garlic, peeled and left
     whole
6 anchovy fillets
1 tablespoon chopped parsley

I love the Union Square Greenmarket, an amazing source of everything vegetable. One of the recent varieties of turnips I've found there are heirloom Japanese button turnips. These are sweet and gorgeous and can be eaten raw or cooked. I love them simply roasted in the oven with sea salt and butter and then tossed with an anchovy butter.

Anchovies make almost anything taste better, and turnips are especially enhanced by their wonderful flavor.

1   Preheat the oven to 425°F (220°C).

2   In a roasting pan, combine ¼ cup (60 ml) water, the turnips, and 2 tablespoons of the butter. Roast for 20 minute, flipping them over halfway through cooking to get nice caramelization on both sides.

3   With a mortar and pestle, crush the garlic, anchovies, parsley, and remaining 2 tablespoons butter to a paste.

4   Place half of the anchovy butter in a bowl, add the hot turnips, leaving the butter in the roasting pan, and toss well. Serve hot. Add more anchovy butter if desired.

RATATOUILLE

Barbuto was to some degree influenced by my travels, and yet in my travels I've never had a good ratatouille; even in Mougins, France, where they claim they do an authentic one. I imagine that the dish has evolved in two pathways—one via home cooks; and the other, a more "sophisticated" restaurant variety. We have deconstructed interpretations, Asian and Indian versions, even an American variety. In my world, I have been taught to sauté the vegetables separately and then merge them; other chefs have advised me to cook in a strict order: onions, garlic, eggplant, zucchini, and so on.

The following is my latest and preferred route to a good ratatouille. It uses a very standard cooking methodology and actually tastes better at room temperature. When hot, it loses some of its earthy subtleties. The caramelization of the vegetables is paramount to success. To achieve this, you must cook at a fairly high temperature. This is a bit nervous-making at first, but the results are worth it. If you can find them, I love the addition of rosemary blossoms, and a little lavender is a delightful touch too.

2 bell peppers
5 tablespoons (75 ml) extra-
   virgin olive oil, divided
2 zucchini, diced
3 Japanese-style eggplants,
   diced
2 onions, diced
3 cloves garlic, peeled and left
   whole
2 large tomatoes, diced
¼ cup (60 ml) Mint Pesto
   (page 251)
Sea salt and freshly ground
   black pepper

1 Grill the peppers over an open flame quickly, 10 to 15 minutes; do not blacken them. Place in a bowl, cover, and let steam for 30 minutes. Destem and peel the peppers and remove as many of the seeds as possible. Cut into dice, reserving the juice.

2 In a large sauté pan, heat 2 tablespoons of the oil over high heat. Sauté the zucchini until richly golden, 8 to 10 minutes. Remove the zucchini from the pan and set aside.

3 Add 2 more tablespoons oil to the pan and cook the eggplant. It is extremely important to cook eggplants all the way, and also avoid burning them. This should take 10 to 15 minutes, depending on the variety. Eggplants vary widely, and they absorb oil like crazy. Remove and mix with the zucchini.

4 Add 1 tablespoon oil and the onions to the pan. Season and cook quicky, about 2 minutes.

5 Lower the heat under the pan and return the zucchini and eggplant to the pan, along with the peppers and tomatoes. Cook gently, uncovered, for 15 minutes or until tender.

6 Stir in the pesto, season with salt and pepper, and serve.

SAUCES, OILS, AND PESTOS

mostarda

MAKES 3 CUPS (850 ML)

1 tablespoon butter

½ shallot, minced

1 clove garlic, peeled and sliced

½ cup (120 ml) white wine

2 tablespoons (30 ml) sherry

¼ cup (40 g) mustard seeds

⅛ teaspoon cayenne pepper

½ cup (100 g) sugar

3 apples, peeled and diced

½ cup (50 g) fresh or frozen cranberries

In a saucepan, add the butter, shallot, and garlic; cook gently over a low heat for 5 minutes. Add the wine, sherry, and mustard seeds.

Simmer the sauce for 10 minutes.

Add the cayenne and sugar; cook another 5 minutes. Add the apples and cranberries and cook, covered, for 40 minutes, until it thickens to a cranberry sauce–like consistency.

tomato sauce

MAKES PLENTY!—10 CUPS (2.8 L)

1 #10 can (102 ounces/2.89 kg) cooked tomatoes

3 tablespoons olive oil

1 onion, peeled and minced

2 tablespoons basil

2 cloves garlic, peeled and sliced

Sea salt

In a 4-quart (3.8 L) saucepan, heat the olive oil over medium heat. Add the onions, basil stems, and garlic. Season with salt and cook gently for 5 minutes. Add the tomatoes and stir well. Bring to a boil, then reduce to a simmer.

Cook for 45 minutes, stirring every 5 minutes.

Remove the basil stems and, using an immersion blender, puree the sauce in the pan.

Store in a glass container. Keeps in the refrigerator for 2 weeks.

aioli

MAKES 1½ CUPS (425 ML)

3 egg yolks

2 tablespoons fresh lemon juice

Sea salt

3 cloves garlic, peeled

1 cup pure olive oil

Finely ground black pepper

In a stand mixer with a whisk attachment, combine the egg yolks, lemon juice, and ¼ teaspoon sea salt.

Smash the garlic with the flat side of a chef's knife and add to the mixer.

Whip for 3 minutes.

With the motor running, slowly drizzle in the olive oil until the mixture achieves a mayo-like consistency.

Add more salt, taste, and add finely ground black pepper.

heirloom tomato salsa

MAKES 4 CUPS (ABOUT 1 L)

1½ pounds (680 g) heirloom tomatoes

4 tablespoons (60 ml) olive oil

3 shallots, not peeled

1 jalapeño, seeded and cut into strips

4 tablespoons (60 ml) sherry vinegar

¾ cup (30 g) chopped fresh cilantro

Sea salt

Preheat the oven to 400°F (205°C). Place the tomatoes on a cookie sheet, skin side down, and drizzle with about 2 teaspoons olive oil. Add the skin-on shallots and jalapeño. Cook for about 25 minutes or until tender. Move the vegetables to a cutting board. Dice the tomatoes, mince the jalapeño, and peel and slice the shallots. Toss the vegetables together in a serving bowl. Add the vinegar, remaining olive oil, and cilantro and stir well. Season with sea salt.

romesco salsa

MAKES 4 CUPS (ABOUT 1 L)

1 large yellow onion, peel on

4 medium heirloom tomatoes

Sea salt

2 tablespoons olive oil, plus more for the casserole

1 jalapeño, seeded and minced

4 cloves garlic, peeled and minced

½ cup (45 g) toasted and crushed hazelnuts

¼ cup (25 g) toasted and crushed almonds

2 teaspoons smoked paprika

2 tablespoons sherry vinegar

2 Calabrian chiles, minced

Preheat the oven to 400°F (205°C). Place onion on a sheet pan and bake for 30 minutes. Let cool. Then peel and slice.

Turn up the oven temperature to 450°F (230°C). Lightly oil a rimmed baking sheet. Core the tomatoes, cut them in half along the equator, and sprinkle each half with sea salt and olive oil. Bake for 20 to 30 minutes or until the tomatoes are golden and wilted.

In a food processor, puree the roasted tomatoes, onions, jalapeño, and garlic.

Add the hazelnuts and almonds, paprika, vinegar, chiles, and olive oil and puree again—the sauce should be a bit rough.

salsa verde

MAKE 3 CUPS (850 ML)

¼ cup (30 g) capers in salt

4 salt-cured anchovies, rinsed and deboned

3 cloves garlic

½ cup (25 g) chopped fresh parsley

½ cup (25 g) chopped arugula

½ cup (20 g) chopped fresh basil

½ cup (20 g) chopped fresh cilantro

¼ cup (13 g) chopped tarragon

¼ cup (11 g) chopped fresh chives

¼ cup (9 g) chopped fresh sage

1 cup (240 ml) extra-virgin olive oil

¼ teaspoon sea salt

Soak the capers in cold water for 1 hour, then drain.

Soak the anchovies in cold water for 15 minutes, then pat dry.

Using a mortar and pestle, smash together the capers, anchovies, and garlic until smooth, then transfer to a large bowl.

Add all the herbs and oil.

Season with salt. It should be chunky, not oily.

salsa picante

MAKES 2 CUPS (500 ML)

3 Fresno chiles

1 jalapeño chile

1 onion, diced

6 cloves garlic, sliced

3 shallots, diced

6 tablespoons (90 ml) olive oil

4 tablespoons (60 ml) red wine vinegar

Sea salt

In a cast-iron skillet over medium-high heat (turn on the fan), toast the chiles, onion, garlic, and shallots.

Keep toasting until golden brown. Transfer to a bowl and cover. Let steam for 1 hour, until the chiles are tender.

Remove the stems and seeds from the chiles and place the chiles, onion, garlic, and shallot in a blender along with the olive oil and vinegar. Pulse until a rough salsa emerges. Season with sea salt.

basil oil

MAKES ¼ CUP (60 ML)

Sea salt

18 fresh basil leaves

4 tablespoons (60 ml) olive oil

In a saucepan, boil 1 quart (945 ml) water with a pinch of salt

Add basil leaves and cook for 3 seconds until just wilted.

Remove the basil with a slotted spoon and immediately rinse basil under a cold stream of water until cool.

Put the basil in a bowl and, using a hand immersion blender, puree the basil with the olive oil and 1 teaspoon of sea salt.

mint pesto

MAKES 1 CUP (235 ML)

6 tablespoons (22 g) hazelnuts

2–3 cloves garlic, peeled

1 cup fresh mint leaves

Sea salt

¾ cup (180 ml) olive oil

6 tablespoons grated Parmesan cheese

Preheat the oven to 350°F (175°C). Toast the hazelnuts in the oven for 10 minutes, or until golden.

In a small food processor, combine the garlic, hazelnuts, and mint. Add 1 teaspoon sea salt. Pulse the machine and dribble in the oil.

Add the Parmesan and pulse once or twice to combine. This will last in the fridge for 2 weeks.

hazelnut pesto

MAKES 1 CUP (235 ML)

3 tablespoons hazelnuts

1½ bunches (about 33 g) fresh basil

1½ spring garlic bulbs

¾ cup (180 ml) olive oil

Sea salt

Preheat the oven to 350°F (175°C). Toast the hazelnuts in the oven for 10 minutes, or until golden.

Let cool, remove the skins if desired, and then lightly crush the nuts.

Bring a saucepan with 2 cups (480 ml) water to a boil, dip the basil in the water for 10 seconds, and then rinse under cold water.

Mince the basil. In a mortar and pestle, combine the garlic, hazelnuts, and basil; mash together and then drizzle in the oil to form a pesto.

Season with salt.

winter pesto

MAKES 1 CUP (235 ML)

½ cup (64 g) pine nuts, toasted in the oven for 8 minutes at 300°F (150°C) and cooled

2–3 cloves garlic, peeled

1 cup (80 g) chopped fresh Italian parsley leaves

¾ cup (120 ml) olive oil

6 tablespoons grated Parmesan cheese

Sea salt and freshly ground black pepper

In a food processor, combine the pine nuts, garlic, and parsley; puree and add the oil.

Add the Parmesan and pulse to combine. Season with salt and pepper.

COCKTAILS

rosé sangria

**MAKES 1 LARGE PITCHER TO SERVE 8
(5 OUNCES/150ML EACH, PLUS ICE)**

We are known for rosé in the summer, so it was natural to offer a refreshing and fun alternative for lunch and brunch service. I love this rosé sangria, and it has become a staple. The recipe has varied over the years, and we try to keep it seasonal. To a base of fruity rosé, fruit liqueur, citrus juice, and the occasional grappa, tequila, or the like, we add seasonal fruit (berries, stone fruit, citrus, and so on) and, last, some club soda.

- 1 (750 ml) bottle dry rosé
- 3 ounces (90 ml) Combier triple sec, or grappa
- 2 ounces (60 ml) fresh lemon juice
- 4 ounces (120 ml) dry citrus soda
- 2 ounces (60 ml) Batavia arrack
- 2 ounces (60 ml) Passion Fruit Syrup (page 258)
- 2 cups (about 260 g) chopped, sliced, or small whole seasonal fruit, plus more for garnish

Combine all the ingredients in a 3-quart (3 L) glass container and chill for at least 1 hour. Serve in large wineglasses filled with ice. Garnish with additional fruit.

1919

MAKES 1 COCKTAIL

This was the first (successful) cocktail that Tynan Cray-craft, Barbuto mixologist extraordinaire, put on the menu and it has remained a bestseller ever since. After starting with Aperol, we decided to move to Cappelletti, probably because we felt it really paired well with the fresh grapefruit juice.

- 1½ ounces Cappelletti Apertivo wine
- 2 ounces fresh grapefruit juice
- 4 to 5 ounces dry prosecco
- Garnish: Grapefruit peel

In a large wineglass filled with ice, mix the Cappelletti, grapefruit juice, and prosecco. Stir and express one large grapefruit peel over the glass. Garnish with the peel.

jw margarita

MAKES 1 COCKTAIL

My bartenders know that before you get behind the bar at Barbuto, you better know how to make a Margarita JW style! Here's what it takes: good tequila, Combier, and fresh-squeezed lime juice. No exceptions.

- 2 ounces premium blanco tequila
- ¾ ounce Combier or comparable orange liqueur (grand Marnier, Cointreau, etc.)
- Juice of 1 lime (about 1 ounce)
- Garnishes: Pink Hawaiian salt, lime wedge (if you like)

In a shaker, combine the tequila, Combier, and lime juice. Shake with ice and strain into a rocks glass rimmed with pink salt and filled with ice. Garnish with a lime wedge.

dr. mcconnack's magical tonic

MAKES 1 COCKTAIL

This is a winter favorite, influenced by traditional cold remedies. Honey, lemon, and turmeric play well with the spicy flavors of the Amaro and bourbon.

- 2 ounces bourbon
- ¾ ounce Turmeric Honey (recipe follows)
- ½ ounce fresh lemon juice
- ½ ounce Amaro Sibilla
- Garnish: Piece of star anise or a lemon round

In a shaker, combine the bourbon, turmeric honey, lemon juice, and amaro. Shake with ice and strain into a rocks glass filled with ice. Garnish with a piece of star anise.

Turmeric Honey

MAKES ABOUT 1½ CUPS (360 ML; 12 OUNCES)

- 1 teaspoon ground turmeric
- 2 teaspoons ground cinnamon
- 1 star anise
- ½ cup (120 ml) honey

Toast the turmeric for 3 minutes in a dry saucepan over low heat. Then add the cinnamon and star anise and cook for 3 minutes or until aromatic. Add 1 cup (240 ml) water and bring up to medium heat, then add the honey. Stir the mixture until thoroughly mixed. Let cool. Strain through a mesh strainer lined with cheesecloth into a clean container.

the poppet

MAKES 1 COCKTAIL

Another perennial favorite. Vodka, lemon juice, and a bit of homemade rosemary syrup topped with club soda makes for a fun cocktail that's not too sweet. Garnishing with a big rosemary sprig adds great aroma and visual flair.

1½ ounces vodka	Club soda
¾ ounce fresh lemon juice	Garnish: Rosemary sprig
¾ ounce Rosemary Syrup (recipe follows)	

In a stainless steel or silver-plated shaker; combine the vodka, lemon juice, and rosemary syrup. Add two scoops of crushed ice. Shake with the ice and then strain into a Collins glass filled with more crushed ice. Top with 1 ounce of club soda. Add a rosemary sprig for garnish.

Rosemary Syrup

MAKES 1 QUART, OR ENOUGH FOR 20 DRINKS

Large handful of fresh rosemary sprigs

2 cups sugar

3 cups cold water

Place the rosemary, sugar, and water in a saucepan and bring to a boil. Reduce and simmer for 5 minutes on medium-low heat. Pour through a mesh strainer and allow to cool.

bank street buck

MAKES 1 COCKTAIL

This is a perfect autumn cocktail. Whiskey, local apple cider, lemon, and spicy ginger beer. The allspice dram adds a lot of depth, with flavors of blackstrap rum and mulling spice.

2 ounces bourbon	2 ounces apple cider
¼ ounce allspice dram	2 ounces ginger beer
½ ounce fresh lemon juice	Garnish: Apple slice

In a shaker, combine the bourbon, allspice dram, lemon juice, and cider. Shake with ice, then pour into an ice-filled Collins glass. Top with the ginger beer and garnish with an apple slice.

aqua fresca

MAKES 1 COCKTAIL

Tynan, Barbuto's brilliant mixologist, tried making an elaborate cocktail with fresh watermelon juice but kept coming up short. After that, he decided to let the fruit speak for itself. Fresh watermelon juice is delightfully delicious and benefits from a hint of acid from the lime juice. Blanco tequila is recommended, but any clear spirit works well.

1½ ounces vodka	½ ounce fresh lime juice
4 ounces Watermelon Juice (recipe follows)	Garnish: Watermelon slice or lime wedges

In a Collins glass filled with ice, pour the tequila, watermelon juice, and lime juice. Stir well, then pour into a rocks glass filled with ice. Garnish with a watermelon slice or wedge of lime.

Watermelon Juice

MAKES ABOUT 4 TO 6 DRINKS

2 cups diced ripe organic watermelon

½ cup (100 g) sugar

Place the watermelon in a blender and add the sugar. Puree, then strain through a mesh strainer.

negroni cativo

MAKES 1 COCKTAIL

Tynan came up with this libation during the weeks leading up to Halloween. He wanted a festive drink, and Negronis were (and still are) very popular. Campari and Cynar bring a lot of bitterness, but it's rounded out by the soft notes of caramel, sarsaparilla, saffron, and spice in the Borsci.

1 ounce Cynar	1 ounce Borsci San Marzano liqueur
1 ounce Campari	Garnish: Orange twist

In a tall mixing glass, combine the Cynar, Campari, and Borsci. Stir for 30 seconds. Strain into a rocks glass filled with ice. Garnish with an orange twist.

the fennel countdown

MAKES 1 COCKTAIL

This is a great drink that Tynan put on the menu a few years ago. It's always nice to offer something with a savory element to offset the more fruity drinks we offer.

2 ounces dry gin

¾ ounce fresh lemon juice

½ ounce honey syrup

2 dashes fennel bitters

½ ounce Don Ciccio & Figli Finocchietto (fennel liqueur)

Garnish: Fennel Salt (recipe follows)

In a shaker, combine the gin, lemon juice, honey syrup, bitters, and Finocchietto. Shake with ice and strain into a martini glass rimmed with fennel salt.

Fennel Salt

MAKES ABOUT 1 CUP (240 GRAMS)

2 tablespoons whole fennel seeds

1 cup (240 g) sea salt

Toast the fennel seeds and salt in a pan over low heat for 8 minutes. Finely grind in a spice mill.

the flats

MAKES 1 COCKTAIL

This cocktail is an ode to our longtime neighbors at Tortilla Flats. When they closed, we devised this beauty to remember the lamented and sorely missed restaurant.

1 or 2 red Fresno chili slices, plus more for garnish

1½ ounces mezcal (we use Agave de Cortes)

1 ounce Passion Fruit Syrup (recipe follows)

½ ounce fresh lime juice

In a shaker, muddle the chili slices. Add the mezcal, passion fruit syrup, and lime juice. Shake with ice and double strain into a rocks glass filled with ice. Garnish with a chili slice.

Passion Fruit Syrup

MAKES 2 CUPS (480 ML; 16 OUNCES)

1 cup (240 ml) unsweetened frozen passion fruit puree

1 cup (240 ml) simple syrup (page 295, minus the lemon)

In a medium bowl, whisk together the ingredients. Keep refrigerated for up to a week.

paloma milano

MAKES 1 COCKTAIL

A Mexican classic with an Italian twist. Michael Kelly, Barbuto's wine director, is responsible for this one.

1½ ounces blanco tequila

½ ounce Campari

1 ounce fresh grapefruit juice

1 ounce grapefruit soda

In a shaker, combine the tequila, Campari, and grapefruit juice. Shake with ice and strain into a highball glass filled with ice. Top with the grapefruit soda.

tempestoso (dark and stormy)

MAKES 1 COCKTAIL

The combination of fresh ginger syrup and amaro adds a new dimension to a classic cocktail.

1½ ounces dark rum

¾ ounce Ginger Syrup (recipe follows)

¾ ounce fresh lime juice

2 ounces ginger beer

Garnish: Lime wedge

In a shaker, combine the rum, ginger syrup, and lime juice. Shake with ice and strain into a highball glass over ice. Top with the ginger beer. Garnish with lime.

Ginger Syrup

MAKES ENOUGH FOR UP TO 18 DRINKS

1 cup (115 g) fresh ginger

½ cup (120 ml) fresh lime juice

2 cups (400 g) sugar

Dice the ginger and add to a food processor. Pulse the ginger until minced. Add 2 cups (480 ml) water and pulse until the mixture is pureed. Add the lime juice and more water (if necessary to ensure the mixture is liquid). Transfer the pureed ginger to a saucepan; add sugar and stir until dissolved. Bring to a boil, then reduce the heat to a slim simmer. Cook for 1 hour. Strain through a mesh strainer and allow to cool.

PASTRY

THIS CHAPTER ON PASTRY is all about Heather Miller and the pastry team at Barbuto. For fifteen years, through a great amount of hard work and glee, they have bolstered the kitchen with a stellar array of simple, delicious pastries. They have had a wonderful time creating and maintaining the rustic and special desserts, breads, and ice creams that warm the hearts of people dining at Barbuto. Heather is the cornerstone of the pastry world at Barbuto, without a doubt the most important person in my pastry universe.

Heather is both my pastry chef and my pastry muse, mentoring others at Barbuto, Jams, and the rest of my organization. The staff speaks with reverence about her, and she is always there, working, thinking, and creating scrumptious concoctions. This chapter would be a sad affair without her influence, recipes, and enthusiasm. Heather's approach has always been idiosyncratic, and she is caring to a fault. She is probably the most underrated pastry chef in America, and she is self-taught!

Heather and I have wonderful talks. She is very funny and alert, but occasionally she gets what we might call a "pastry block." It happens to the best of us. If I sense this, and her daily grind has worn her out a bit, we talk seasonality. Since I have a good retention for what is available (or should be) at any time of year, I begin our talk with a subject like blueberries or Concord grapes or pears. Then we move on to discuss plums, apricots, peaches, nectarines, and so on. From these explorations, she begins to talk shop. "What about this or that?" she will suggest. My job is to encourage her inherent creativity and let the pastry juices flow. It is my greatest joy.

BISCOTTI

MAKES 30 BISCOTTI

3 tablespoons (50 g) almond
    paste
3 tablespoons (40 g) butter,
    softened
1¾ cups (350 g) sugar
Zest of 4 oranges
3 large eggs
1½ teaspoons vanilla extract
1½ teaspoons almond extract
2¾ cups (330 g) all-purpose
    flour
1½ teaspoon baking powder
¾ teaspoon salt
5 cups (675 g) hazelnuts and
    whole almonds, toasted,
    roughly chopped, and
    mixed together

My paternal grandmother was a very sweet and hard-working person. She toiled in the garment industry in Manhattan her whole adult life, work that rendered her hands arthritic and gnarled. And yet she did it without complaint. I did not know her well, as my father had decided to live on the West Coast—which must have been difficult for him, as he really loved and respected his mom. As for me, other than a sweaty July visit to New York when I was thirteen, I had no real knowledge of her. But one thing stuck with me: her mandelbrot. These not-so-sweet, addictive morsels were her version of biscotti. Twice baked, with a delicate crunch, they were made with love.

1   Preheat the oven to 350°F (175°C).

2   In the bowl of an electric mixer, beat the almond paste; slowly add the butter and sugar until combined with no lumps of almond paste.

3   Add the orange zest, and then add the eggs one at a time until incorporated. Add the vanilla and almond extracts. Add all the dry ingredients, then stir in the nuts.

4   Shape into seven logs and place on a sheet pan. Bake until firm to the touch, about 20 minutes. Lower the oven temperature to 300°F (150°C).

5   Slice the loaves into ¾-inch (2 cm) slices and lay them out on a sheet pan. Bake for 10 to 15 minutes, then remove and let cool.

6   If the cookies are not thoroughly crunchy, put them back in the oven for a few minutes. Don't let the cookies brown; just dry them out until crispy.

PEACH AND BLUEBERRY CROSTATAS

SERVES 8

A crostata is a sweet tart in the Italian baking canon. At Barbuto we like the presentation to be more rustic than that of a formal fruit tart. Crostatas are probably the most important pastry that we serve. We might sell more budino and tiramisus, but crostatas are the mainstay. We follow the seasons. Among the most popular crostatas are apple, peaches, plum, pear, apricot, and strawberry. I'm a huge fan of bush berries; in particular, I really love raspberries, black-berries, blueberries, boysenberries, and loganberries.

The crust is so important here. We like individual crostatas. The pastry is like a delicate flower, so we need to be careful, deliberate and not work the pastry too hard. Gluten really is not our friend here; a tough dough makes for a terrible pastry crust.

Here are some tricks of the trade used to combat the effects of gluten. First of all, keep all the ingredients as cold as possible; secondly, work as quickly as possible; and third, make sure that you're not working on a day that is too hot. I like to freeze all the components ahead of time; it really helps to protect the dough from becoming tight, stiff, and indelicate. *recipe continues*

FOR THE CRUST:

3¾ cups (400 g) pastry flour
3 tablespoons (35 g) sugar
1½ teaspoons salt
1½ cups (340 g) butter, cold,
 cut into ½-inch (12 mm)
 cubes
¾ cup (180 ml) ice water

FOR THE FILLING:

About 8 peaches, pitted and
 quartered
2 cups (290 g) blueberries
Juice of ½ lemon
2 tablespoons sugar

TO BAKE:

1 egg
1 teaspoon sugar

1   Make the crust: In the bowl of an electric mixer, combine the flour, sugar, and salt.

2   Add the butter and mix with the paddle attachment for 4 to 5 minutes on low speed, until the butter chunks are about one-quarter of their original size.

3   Add the ice water all at once and mix for just another 30 seconds, until the water is incorporated but the dough is still rough and shaggy.

4   Remove the dough, form into a disc, and wrap in plastic wrap. Chill for several hours or up to 3 days.

5   When you are ready to make the crostatas, roll the dough on a floured surface to about ⅛ inch (3 mm) thick. Cut into 5-inch (12 cm) squares.

6   Make the filling: In a bowl, toss the peaches and blueberries with the lemon juice and sugar.

7   Cut parchment paper into 5-inch (12 cm) squares.

8   Scoop about ½ cup (120 ml) of the filling onto the middle of each pastry square and fold up the corners. Place each crostata onto a square of parchment and place in a cup of a muffin pan.

9   Chill the crostatas for 1 hour or until you are ready to bake them.

10   Preheat the oven to 400°F (205°C). Beat the egg with the sugar.

11   Brush the exposed dough of the crostatas with the egg and sprinkle with sugar.

12   Bake for 30 to 35 minutes, until the peaches are bubbly and the crust is deep golden in color. Serve.

GIANDUJA SOUFFLÉ

SERVES 8

8 eggs
1 cup (240 ml) heavy cream
½ cup (90 g) chopped
    bittersweet chocolate
½ cup (70 g) toasted
    hazelnuts
2 tablespoons grappa
½ cup (1 stick/115 g) butter,
    plus more for the mold
2 tablespoons pastry flour
¼ cup (50 g) sugar, plus more
    for the baking dish
¼ teaspoon cream of tartar
⅛ teaspoon sea salt
½ teaspoon vanilla extract
1 teaspoon confectioners'
    sugar
1 teaspoon cocoa powder

Barbuto—soufflé? Well, why not? They are fun, spectacular, and delicious. They are also a must for any home cook to master. When I was the chef at Michael's in Santa Monica forty years ago, we always featured both Grand Marnier and chocolate soufflés on the menu. You will not find a soufflé every day at Barbuto—but you never know.

1   Preheat the oven to 375°F (190°C). Butter a soufflé mold and coat with sugar, tapping out any extra.

2   Separate the eggs. Place the whites in the bowl of a stand mixer and set aside the yolks.

3   In a saucepan, combine ½ cup (120 ml) of the cream, the chocolate, hazelnuts, and grappa. Bring to a simmer. When the mixture has thickened, using an immersion blender, puree the contents of the saucepan; this is the gianduja.

4   In a second saucepan on the stove, combine 2 tablespoons of the butter, the flour, and 1 tablespoon of the sugar and cook over low heat for 5 minutes, stirring constantly. Add the egg yolks. Remove from the heat. Add the hazelnut gianduja and mix well. Let cool.

5   Whip the egg whites with the cream of tartar to a soft peak, then slowly add the remaining sugar and whip until stiff but not dry-looking. Fold the whites into the gianduja–egg yolk mixture and add the salt and vanilla extract.

6   Whip the remaining ½ cup (120 ml) cream with the confectioners' sugar and set aside.

7   Fill the mold with the soufflé mixture. Bake for 20 minutes, or until doubled in size. Dust with cocoa powder. Serve with the whipped cream.

STRAWBERRY PAVLOVAS

SERVES 6 TO 8

I'm a huge fan of English pastries. I love them all; fresh strawberries and heavy cream, apple pie, treacle pie, short-bread cookies, brownies, and the like. And the delicious pavlova (though it's technically an Australian concoction).

I thought it was a perfect fit for Barbuto. What's better than a crunchy meringue, with a soft, tender center, topped with freshly whipped cream, warm seasonal fruit, powdered sugar, and more whipped cream? It took forever for my chefs at Barbuto to understand this recipe. For some reason, they were convinced that the meringue had to be hard all the way through. In fact, they need to be tender in the center, crunchy on the exterior, light and delicate. This is an easy recipe to achieve greatness; the only thing you need to realize is that the meringues cannot cook too long, nor at too high a temperature. It also helps if your oven is calibrated, and that you use a nonstick surface when cooking your meringues.

Note: This recipe should make about eight meringues, so don't worry if some crack or break when you pick them up—you'll have plenty! Be sure to use them the same day you make them, but don't assemble the pavlovas until just before you serve them. *recipe continues*

FOR THE MERINGUES:

5 egg whites (150 ml)
¼ teaspoon cream of tartar
⅞ cup (175 g) sugar
2 teaspoons cornstarch
½ teaspoon apple cider
vinegar
½ teaspoon vanilla extract

FOR THE FILLING:

2 cups (290 g) strawberries,
sliced
1 teaspoon Grand Marnier
1 teaspoon grated orange zest
1 tablespoon fresh orange
juice
1 cup (240 ml) heavy cream,
whipped

1   Make the meringues: Preheat the oven to 225°F (110°C).

2   Line a cookie sheet with parchment paper or silicone liners.

3   Put the egg whites and cream of tartar in the bowl of an electric mixer.

4   Using the whip attachment, whip the whites on medium speed until frothy. Begin adding sugar, about 2 tablespoons at a time, whipping for 30 to 40 seconds between each addition.

5   When all the sugar has been added, whip until the whites form stiff peaks and are glossy.

6   Add the cornstarch, vinegar, and vanilla and mix until just combined.

7   Gently spoon blobs of meringue onto the lined pans, in circles about 3 inches (7.5 cm) in diameter and 2 inches (5 cm) tall. With the back of a spoon, make a dent in the center of each meringue so there is a place to hold the filling, and leave an inch or two of space between meringues. Bake for 1 hour, then turn off the oven and leave the meringues to cool in the oven. Ideally they will be pale white and crispy outside with a soft, creamy center.

8   Put the meringues on individual serving plates.

9   Make the filling: Toss together the strawberries (or fruit of your choice), orange liqueur, orange zest, and orange juice. Let the strawberries sit for 1 hour to absorb the juices.

10 Mound the strawberries on top of the meringues then top with plain whipped cream and serve.

SHORTCAKE WITH BERRIES

SERVES 8

FOR THE BISCUITS:

2 cups (240 g) all-purpose
  flour
½ cup (80 g) polenta
¼ cup (50 g) sugar, plus more
  for baking
1 tablespoon baking powder
1 teaspoon salt
1½ cups (355 ml) heavy
  cream, plus more for
  baking

TO SERVE:

1 cup (240 ml) heavy cream
1 tablespoon sugar
2 cups (290 g) of the best
  strawberries you can find
2 cups (290 g) blueberries
1 tablespoon confectioners'
  sugar

I love simplicity, and this is it: a recipe for every day, a recipe that will make our lives just a little bit better. The use of white grits is an ode both to America and to Italy (polenta). The cornmeal adds nuttiness and texture to the cake. It also gives a certain silkiness that flour alone cannot provide. And for any non-gluten fans, the fine white grits can be used 100 percent instead of the flour.

1   Preheat the oven to 375°F (190°C).

2   Mix the flour, polenta, baking powder, sugar, and salt. Add the cream and mix by hand until a rough dough forms. Empty the contents onto the countertop and knead a few times until the dough holds together.

3   Roll the dough out to 1 inch (2.5 cm) thick. Cut into 3-inch (7.5 cm) rounds. Brush with 1 tablespoon cream and sprinkle with 1 tablespoon sugar. Place on a baking sheet and bake for 15 to 20 minutes, or until golden brown. Let cool.

4   Clean and slice the strawberries, mix with the blueberries in a bowl, add 2 tablespoons sugar, and toss well.

5   Whip 1 cup (240 ml) heavy cream with the remaining 1 tablespoon sugar.

6   Split the cakes in half, place ¼ cup (60 ml) of the berries and a dollop of whipped cream on each. Dust with confectioners' sugar and serve.

BUDINO

(4-OUNCE
PORTIONS)**

8 ounces plus 1 ounce (225 g)
  dark chocolate (reserve
  the 1 ounce for garnish)
8 ounces (225 g) milk
  chocolate
2½ cups (480 ml) heavy
  cream, divided
8 egg yolks
1 cup plus 1 tablespoon
  (200 g) sugar
6 tablespoons (85 g) butter,
  softened
Pinch of salt
1 tablespoon plus 1 teaspoon
  Kahlúa
1 teaspoon powdered sugar

Budino is the most popular of Barbuto's dessert offerings. It is the perfect ending to a Barbuto meal: rich and delicate at the same time. *Budino* is simply "pudding" in Italian. The puddings of my youth came from a box, but I loved them just the same. This decadent big brother has all the fixings: rich chocolate, sugar, cream, and butter—a far more advanced version of the boxed one my mom served in the mid-1950s.

There is a version of this in my prevous book *Italian My Way*. This differs in a few ways; it has booze, it has more milk chocolate, and it is a better version!

1   The easiest method to melt/temper chocolate (thank you Richard Grausman, Cordon Bleu circa 1974!): Place the chocolates in a stainless-steel or copper bowl. Heat 3 cups of water to a simmer. Turn off the heat, wait 5 minutes, then carefully pour the heated water over the chocolate.

2   Let sit for 2 minutes, then carefully pour off the water in the sink. The chocolate will be tempered.

3   Warm 1½ cups cream in a heavy saucepan set over low heat for 2 minutes.

4   In a bowl, whisk together the egg yolks and the sugar.

5   Add the heated cream into the egg yolks; dribble in slowly, stirring with a wooden spoon as you go.

6   Pour the egg yolk mixture back into the saucepan and cook over low heat, stirring constantly, until the mixture thickens slightly and coats the back of the spoon.

7   Stir in the butter. Let the mixture cool in the pan.

8 Use a whisk to add the egg yolk mixture little by little into the chocolate. Add ¼ teaspoon sea salt and 1 tablespoon Kahlúa. Taste.

9 Portion the pudding into 8-ounce coffee cups or glass jars. Fill halfway, or 4 ounces per.

10 In the bowl of an electric mixer, or in a large bowl using a hand mixer, whip 1 cup of cream, then add 1 tablespoon sugar and 1 teaspoon Kahlúa. Top each cup or glass with a dollop of whipped cream.

11 To serve: using a vegetable peeler, scrape the 1 tablespoon dark chocolate over the cream.

12 Dust with powdered sugar.

LEMON-PISTACHIO CAKE

SERVES 12 TO 14

FOR THE LEMON-MASCARPONE CREAM:

Zest of 1 lemon
1 cup (240 ml) heavy cream
½ cup (120 ml) mascarpone
1½ tablespoons sugar
½ teaspoon vanilla extract
Pinch of salt

FOR THE PISTACHIO GENOISE CAKE:

3 ounces (85 g) almond paste
1½ cups (300 g) plus
    2 tablespoons sugar
6 whole eggs
4 egg yolks
½ teaspoon vanilla extract
¼ teaspoon almond extract
1 cup plus 2 tablespoons
    (135 g) cake flour
¼ teaspoon sea salt
1 cup (115 g) pistachio flour
½ cup (120 ml) clarified
    butter, melted and cooled
    (see Note on page 276)
ingredients continue

Here is a cake that Heather designed in a fit of pastry passion a few years ago. It has evolved over time and we are all the beneficiaries of that passion.

It combines the techniques for a special pistachio genoise, a luscious lemon curd, and a sinuous mascarpone cream. These creative recipes are all important to understand and master. Having these recipes as go-tos is a nice confidence builder, too. The cake is a tour de force, and though it is somewhat labor-intensive, it is well worth the effort.

1   For the lemon-mascarpone cream: Heat the lemon zest and cream until hot. Remove from the heat, let cool to room temperature, then refrigerate overnight. Strain the cream and squeeze all the cream out of the zest.

2   Make the pistachio genoise cake: Preheat the oven to 375°F (190°C). Bring a small pot of water to a boil. Grease a half sheet pan and line it with parchment.

3   Using the paddle attachment, beat the almond paste in a stand mixer and very slowly add 1½ cups (300 g) sugar, the eggs, and yolks, stopping and scraping the sides often to make sure there are no almond paste lumps.

4   When all the sugar and eggs are incorporated, remove the bowl from the mixer and whisk over boiling water until warm to the touch.

5   Return the bowl to the mixer, switch to the whip attachment, and whip on medium-high speed until very thick and pale. Add the vanilla and almond extract. *recipe continues*

FOR THE LEMON CURD:

⅓ cup (80 ml) fresh lemon
    juice
Zest of 2 lemons
⅓ cup (65 g) sugar
1 whole egg
1 egg yolk
Pinch of salt

FOR THE VANILLA SYRUP:

½ cup (100 g) sugar
1 teaspoon vanilla extract

TO SERVE:

Pistachio flour or chopped
    pistachios

*Note: To make clarified butter,
    microwave it for 2 minutes on
    high and skim off the foam.*

6   Remove from the mixer, transfer to a big mixing bowl, and sift in the cake flour, the remaining 2 tablespoons sugar, and the salt, gently folding in the dry ingredients.

7   Fold in the pistachio flour, then add about 1 cup (240 ml) batter to the clarified butter, combine gently but thoroughly, then combine with the rest of the batter.

8   Pour into the half sheet pan. Bake for 10 to 12 minutes, until the cake springs back when touched. Let the cake cool completely, then turn it out of the pan.

9   Make the lemon curd: Whisk everything but the salt together in a heatproof bowl.

10   Set the bowl over boiling water and whisk gently but constantly until thick. Strain, add the salt, and chill with plastic wrap directly on top of the curd.

11   Make the lemon mascarpone cream: Put the mascarpone and sugar in the bowl of an electric mixer with the whip attachment. Add about ½ cup (120 ml) of the lemon cream and whip on medium-low speed until no lumps of mascarpone remain.

12   Add the remaining cream, the vanilla, and salt and whip until just thick and spreadable. Do not over-whip or your cream will become grainy-tasting.

13   Make the vanilla syrup: Bring ½ cup (120 ml) water and the sugar to a boil. Remove from the heat, let cool to room temperature, and stir in the vanilla.

14   Assemble the cake: Split the cake in half horizontally. Sprinkle half of the vanilla syrup on the bottom layer to moisten it. Spread a very thin layer of lemon curd over the cake, then a layer of lemon mascarpone cream.

15   Repeat with the second layer, finishing with cream on the top. Wrap the cake and chill until it is set.

16   To serve, sprinkle with pistachio flour or chopped pistachios and cut into slices.

CARAMEL ICE CREAM

MAKES 1 QUART ICE CREAM (SERVES UP TO 8)

1½ cups (300 g) sugar
1 cup (240 ml) heavy cream
1 cup (240 ml) whole milk
½ teaspoon vanilla extract
4 egg yolks
¼ teaspoon salt

Caramel ice cream? It might be my favorite. Years ago at the now forgotten, mythical restaurant Girardet (near Lausanne in Switzerland), I tasted a caramel ice cream unlike any I had ever experenced. It was almost burnt, just on the edge, so that bitterness countered the sweetness in a manner that I found extraordinary. That velvety scoop of caramel ice cream might have been the best dessert—no, the best morsel of food—I had ever tasted. It lingered in a fashion that made it easy to conjure up the nuances, even years later. The trick is to truly darken the caramel till it just seems impossibly dark and bitter, but not burned. This may take a few tries, but persevere. The results are worth the effort.

1 In a heavy copper or stainless-steel pan, cook the sugar to a dark caramel color—do not stir! Add the cream, then the milk and vanilla, and whisk gently.

2 Place the egg yolks in a bowl.

3 Temper the yolks with a bit of the hot liquid. Then pour the mixture with the rest of the liquid into another heavy pan. Make an anglaise, cooking very gently, then add the salt.

4 Strain and chill. Freeze in an ice cream maker according to the manufacturer's instructions.

CHOCOLATE-BROWN BUTTER TART

SERVES 8

FOR THE TART SHELL:

2¾ cups (350 g) all-purpose
    flour, plus more for dusting
½ cup (100 g) sugar
1 cup (225 g) unsalted butter,
    cold, cut into ½-inch
    pieces
2 egg yolks
¼ cup (60 ml) heavy cream

FOR THE FILLING:

3 eggs
1¼ cups (250 g) sugar
½ cup (65 g) all-purpose flour
1 vanilla bean
¾ cup (170 g) unsalted butter
1 cup (170 g) chocolate bits
    (I like to take a bittersweet
    chocolate bar and chop it
    into ¼-inch chunkettes)
1 cup (135 g) hazelnuts,
    toasted for 8 minutes in a
    350°F (175°C) oven

I have been making this recipe in one form or the other for almost forty years. It is an incredibly versatile, straightforward, and delicious recipe. It can really transform any fruit, nut, chocolate, or other sweet item into a fabulous dessert. The person who's really perfected this recipe is my dear friend Nancy Silverton. Nancy might be the most talented, humble, and exciting chef in the world. Her skill sets are numerous—she can bake, she can make cheese, she's an amazing bread maker, and she can do wonders with pizza, pasta, and anything else in the Italian culinary lexicon. Her honesty and intelligence are infectious. This recipe would be nothing without her constant tinkering, adjusting the ingredients over the years in order to create near perfection.

1   Make the tart shell: Combine the flour, sugar, and butter in the bowl of a stand mixer fitted with the paddle attachment. Mix on medium speed until the butter and dry ingredients form a coarse cornmeal consistency, about 2 minutes. (Alternatively, combine the flour, sugar, and butter in a large bowl and, with your fingertips or pastry cutter, crumble into a coarse cornmeal consistency.)

2   Whisk the egg yolks and cream together in a small bowl and add to the flour mixture; mix on low until large chunks form.

3   Turn the dough onto a clean work surface dusted with flour. Press the dough with the heel of your hand and gather the pieces together to bring the dough into a ball.

recipe continues

4   Knead the dough a few more minutes, form it into a disc, wrap tightly with plastic wrap, and chill for at least 1 hour and up to 3 days. This dough makes enough for two 10-inch (25 cm) tarts. (The dough can also be frozen for up to 2 months. Before using, thaw overnight in the refrigerator.)

5   Line a baking sheet with parchment paper or a silicone liner and butter the inside of a 10-inch (25 cm) tart ring; place the ring on the baking sheet.

6   Take the dough out of the refrigerator and cut it in half; reserve one half for later use. Cut the dough into large chunks. Pound the dough with a rolling pin and then knead it a few times to temper the dough to the consistency of Play-Doh.

7   Dust your work surface and rolling pin with flour and pound the dough into a large disc, about ¼ inch (6 mm) thick. Roll the dough out to at least 2 inches (5 cm) larger than the ring to a thickness of ⅛ inch (3 mm). Place the tart ring on top and trim the dough so that 2 inches (5 cm) remain around it. (Discard or use the excess dough scraps as cookie dough.) Brush off the extra flour from the dough. Wrap the dough around the rolling pin and ease it into the tart ring. Dip the knuckle of your index finger in flour and press the dough into the crease with your knuckle so you have a straight edge, not sloping sides. Don't stretch the dough to fit, because it will shrink during baking. Roll your rolling pin over the top of the tart ring to neatly cut off the excess dough; pull off the trimmed dough and discard. Place the tart shell in the refrigerator to chill for at least 30 minutes and up to 1 day.

8   Make the filling: Whisk the eggs and sugar in a large bowl until smooth; add the flour and whisk until thoroughly combined.

9 Using a small, sharp knife, split the vanilla bean lengthwise; scrape out the pulp and seeds and smear them on the butter.

10 Add the butter, vanilla pulp and seeds, and vanilla bean to a small, heavy-bottomed saucepan and heat over high heat until the butter is brown and foamy.

11 Continue cooking the butter until it is dark brown and gives off a nutty aroma. Pour the butter in a slow, steady stream into the bowl with the egg yolks, whisking constantly.

12 When still warm, stir in the chocolate bits and hazelnuts.

13 Remove the vanilla bean. (The filling can be prepared up to 10 days in advance and refrigerated in an airtight container. Just before using, bring it to room temperature until it is a spreadable consistency.)

14 Bake the tart: Adjust the oven rack to the middle position and preheat to 350°F (175°C).

15 Remove the prepared tart shell from the refrigerator.

16 Spoon in the filling to reach about halfway up the sides of the tart and spread evenly.

17 Bake the tart until the top is golden brown, 30 to 40 minutes if you are using an 8-inch (20 cm) ring or 45 minutes if you are using a 10-inch (25 cm) ring. Remove the tart from the oven and allow it to cool completely, or for at least 2 hours.

18 Serve with whipped cream if you like.

CHOCOLATE SHORTBREAD

MAKES ABOUT 48 1½-INCH SQUARE COOKIES

1 cup (225 g) organic unsalted butter
7 tablespoons (95 g) brown sugar
7 tablespoons (85 g) granulated sugar
½ teaspoon vanilla extract
2 ounces (55 g) dark chocolate, melted (preferably a high-quality brand like Jacques Torres)
1¾ cups (210 g) all-purpose flour
¼ cup (25 g) organic Dutch cocoa powder, sifted
¼ teaspoon kosher salt
½ teaspoon Maldon salt

My favorite snack or indulgence is shortbread cookies. One of the greatest treats in the world are chocolate-flavored shortbreads. These are a perfect way to end a meal at Barbuto. Order an espresso, shortbread cookies, and a glass of sweet Tuscan white wine. Perfection.

1 Preheat the oven to 350°F (175°C).

2 Cream the butter and sugars. I like to use a stand mixer fitted with the paddle attachment.

3 Add the vanilla and melted chocolate and mix.

4 Add the flour, cocoa powder, and kosher salt and mix until just incorporated. Roll out the dough about ¼ inch thick.

5 Cut into desired shapes and sprinkle with a little Maldon salt. Place on a cookie sheet, at least 2 inches apart to leave space for the cookies to expand. Bake until crisp through, 12 to 15 minutes.

MILK CHOCOLATE SPRITZ

MAKES 24 COOKIES

½ cup (115 g) unsalted
    butter, plus more for
    the cookie sheet
⅓ cup (65 g) sugar
1 egg yolk
1 cup (125 g) organic
    all-purpose flour
Pinch of sea salt
1½ teaspoons vanilla extract
1½ ounces (40 g) milk
    chocolate
1 tablespoon heavy cream

I happen to love the spritz cookies of the Alps and Dolomites. These butter cookies are infectious and really bad for you! They are truly fun to make, and you will be amazed at people's response. They will think you are a professional baker.

1   Preheat the oven to 375°F (190°C). Butter a cookie sheet.

2   Using a stand mixer fitted with the paddle attachment, combine the butter and sugar and slowly beat them until fluffy. Add the egg yolk and beat, then sprinkle in the flour and salt, beat until fluffy, and add the vanilla.

3   Use a fluted pastry bag to pipe out cookies about 1 inch (2.5 cm) wide and 2 inches (5 cm) long onto the cookie sheet. Bake until they are lightly golden. Let cool completely.

4   Heat the chocolate and cream in a saucepan and whisk until sauce-like.

5   Dip each cookie into the chocolate sauce and then let cool on a rack.

6   To store, keep dry in a sealed glass container, or freeze.

COCONUT-NUT TEACAKES

SERVES 8

1 cup (225 g) butter, softened
½ cup (100 g) granulated
    sugar
1 teaspoon vanilla extract
1¾ cups (225 g) plus
    2 tablespoons all-purpose
    flour
½ teaspoon salt
⅓ cup (30 g) toasted and
    ground almonds
⅓ cup (30 g) toasted and
    ground hazelnuts
⅓ cup (30 g) ground
    desiccated coconut
Confectioners' sugar for
    coating

Here's a terrific recipe, one that encompasses all the attributes of a great cookie. This freezes well, both raw and cooked, so for a party, one can easily thaw some dough, preheat the oven, and in no time at all have delicious cookies.

1   Preheat the oven to 350°F (175°C).

2   In an electric mixer, using the paddle attachment, cream the butter and granulated sugar until fluffy.

3   Add the vanilla, and then add the flour, salt, ground almonds and hazelnuts, and coconut.

4   Roll tablespoons of the dough into balls and place on a cookie sheet. Bake for 10 to 12 minutes, until lightly browned.

5   Let the cookies cool and then roll them in confectioners' sugar.

STRAWBERRY LAYER CAKE

MAKES 7 CAKES

**FOR THE PLAIN
GENOISE CAKE:**

3 eggs
2 yolks
½ cup (100 g) plus
    1 tablespoon sugar
1 tablespoon vanilla extract
⅔ cup (85 g) cake flour
¼ teaspoon salt
4 tablespoons (60 ml) clarified
    butter, cooled (see Note)

**FOR THE MASCARPONE
CREAM:**

½ cup (120 ml) mascarpone
    (1 small tub)
1½ tablespoons sugar, plus
    more to taste
1 cup (240 ml) heavy cream
1 teaspoon vanilla extract
Pinch of sea salt

FOR THE VANILLA SYRUP:

½ cup (100 g) sugar
1 teaspoon vanilla extract

TO ASSEMBLE:

Sliced strawberries

*Note: To make clarified butter,
microwave it for 2 minutes
on high and skim off the
foam.*

I am a total sucker for any layer cake. At my restaurant Adele's in Nashville, I have a coconut cake that is light and ethereal and thoroughly addictive. At Barbuto, we generally like simpler desserts, and this cake exemplifies that philosophy. Try strawberries from the local farmer's market. The season is short, so be on the lookout. Of course, one can use blackberries, raspberries, or blueberries, or a nice combo thereof.

1 Make the plain genoise cake: Preheat the oven to 375°F (190°C). Grease a half sheet pan and line it with parchment paper. Bring a small pot of water to a boil.

2 Put the whole eggs, yolks, and ½ cup (200 g) of the sugar in the bowl of a stand mixer and use a handheld eclectic mixer to whip with a whisk over the boiling water until warm to the touch.

3 Put the bowl on the mixer and using the whip attachment, whip on medium-high speed until very thick and pale. Add the vanilla.

4 Remove from the mixer, transfer to a big mixing bowl, and sift in the flour, remaining 1 tablespoon sugar, and the salt, gently folding in the dry ingredients.

5 In a separate bowl, combine about 1 cup (240 ml) of the batter with the clarified butter, combine gently but thoroughly, and then combine with the rest of the batter. Pour into the prepared half sheet pan. Bake for 10 to 12 minutes, until the cake springs back when touched. *recipe continues*

6   Let the cake cool completely, then turn it out of the pan.

7   Make the mascarpone cream: Put the mascarpone and sugar in the bowl of an electric mixer with the whip attachment.

8   Add about ½ cup (120 ml) of the cream and whip on medium-low speed until no lumps of mascarpone remain.

9   Add the remaining ½ cup (120 ml) cream, the vanilla, and salt and whip until just thick and spreadable. Do not overwhip, or your cream will become grainy and greasy tasting.

10   Make the vanilla syrup: Bring ½ cup (120 ml) water and the sugar to a boil. Remove from the heat, cool to room temp and add the vanilla.

11   Assemble the cake: Cut the cake into as many 3-inch (7.5 cm) circles as you can using a round cookie cutter.

12   Sprinkle each circle with a little vanilla syrup, then spread a dollop of mascarpone cream over half of them. Top each cake with one of the remaining circles.

13   Spoon a dollop of mascarpone cream on top and then some sliced strawberries or fruit of your choice. Serve.

CHOCOLATE MERINGUE COOKIES

MAKES 24 COOKIES

⅔ cup (165 ml) egg whites
2 tablespoons plus ½ cup
    sugar
¼ teaspoon vanilla extract
⅓ cocoa powder
¼ cup (30 g) confectioners'
    sugar
2 tablespoons castor sugar
Pinch of salt
1 tablespoon grated
    unsweetened chocolate

If ever there was a reason to succumb to a chocolate passion, these are it. I wanted to create a chocolate cookie that was different—light, silky, and chocolatey. The chocolate needs to be able to scream its name yet maintain a delicate and luxurious taste. These are perfect as a late-night snack. If you have a need for a nightcap at Barbuto, order an espresso and a plate of these cookies—pure magic.

1   Preheat the oven to 225°F (110°C).

2   In a stand mixer fitted with the whip attachment, whip the egg whites until frothy. Add 2 tablespoons of the sugar and whip to soft peaks. Slowly add the remaining ½ cup (100 g) sugar. Whip until stiff. Whip in the vanilla.

3   Sift together the cocoa powder, confectioners' sugar, castor sugar, and pinch of salt. Fold into the whites, then fold in the grated chocolate.

4   Pipe or spread onto a baking sheet and bake for ½ to 1 hour, depending on the thickness of your cookies. To test, remove one from the oven and let it cool completely. When warm, the meringues will be soft to the touch, but they will crisp up when cool.

TIRAMISU

SERVES 10

2 cups (480 ml) brewed
    espresso or strong coffee
1½ cups (360 ml) Kahlúa
1½ cups (360 ml) mascarpone
Seeds of ½ vanilla bean
¼ cup (50 g) sugar
1¼ cups (300 ml) heavy
    cream
½ teaspoon vanilla extract
Tiny pinch of salt
About 24 ladyfingers
Bittersweet chocolate shavings
    (optional)

Here is a perennial favorite in all Italian restaurants. I have modified this from the one in *Italian My Way* to reflect how recipes evolve.

1   Heat the espresso, ½ cup (120 ml) water, and the Kahlúa in a saucepan. Keep warm.

2   Put the mascarpone, vanilla bean seeds, and sugar in the bowl of an electric mixer with the whip attachment.

3   Add about ½ cup (120 ml) of the cream and whip on medium-low speed until no lumps of mascarpone remain. Add the remaining ¾ cup (180 ml) cream and the salt and whip until just thick and spreadable. Do not overwhip or your cream will become grainy and greasy-tasting.

4   Dip ladyfingers two at a time in the espresso liquid. You don't need to keep them in the liquid for long, just submerge them and take them out again. Place them in the bottom of a 9-inch (23 cm) square baking pan or pie dish (anything with a side). Continue dipping until the bottom of your pan is covered with a solid single layer of ladyfingers.

5   Spread half of the mascarpone cream over the ladyfingers, and then repeat with the remaining ladyfingers and cream.

6   Cover and refrigerate for at least 4 hours. To serve, shave bittersweet chocolate (if using) over the top and cut into squares.

APRICOT CHARLOTTE

SERVES 4

12 ounces (340 g) fresh
    apricots, pitted and sliced
½ cup (120 ml) moscato
11 tablespoons (140 g)
    granulated sugar, plus
    more for baking pan
5 tablespoons butter, softened,
    plus more for baking pan
10 to 15 slices ciabatta, crusts
    removed and slightly stale
Confectioners' sugar for
    dusting

This dates back to my days in Paris, but it truly is a universal recipe—almost every cuisine has a version. Really, it's a type of bread pudding with fruit. This plain Jane recipe will delight, as it is truly bulletproof and works every time.

1   In a saucepan over medium heat, poach the apricots for 10 minutes in the moscato and granulated sugar.

2   Remove the apricots from the heat and set aside.

3   Preheat the oven to 375°F. Butter a 9-inch (23 cm) Pyrex pie plate and coat with sugar, tapping out any extra.

4   Butter each piece of ciabatta on both sides. Dust the buttered ciabatta with confectioners' sugar.

5   Lay some of the bread in the pie plate so that the pieces are overlapping and poke above the edge of the pie plate. Spoon the apricots into the pie plate. Cover the apricots with the remaining bread and press the bread into the apricots.

6   Bake for 30 to 35 minutes, until the ciabatta is golden brown.

7   Allow to cool. Serve with scoops of whipped cream or caramel ice cream (page 277).

LIMONCELLO GRANITA WITH BERRIES

SERVES 6 TO 8

1 cup (240 ml) fresh lemon
    juice (from about 8
    lemons)
⅔ cup (165 ml) limoncello
1 cup (240 ml) lemon simple
    syrup, plus more to taste
    (see Note)
Zest of 2 lemons
Tiny pinch of salt
Sliced strawberries or berries
    of choice
Sugar to taste
Fresh basil

*Note: To make lemon simple
    syrup: Combine 1 cup
    (200 g) sugar, 1 cup
    (240 ml) water, and
    the zest of 1 lemon in a
    saucepan and bring to a
    boil. Remove from the heat
    and let cool completely.*

One November many years ago I ventured to the seaside resort of Positano on the Amalfi Coast. There, in the early winter, the town was tame and tranquil. There were a few tourists about, but mainly the townsfolk had the place to themselves. As we wandered around the hilly village, I noticed that limoncello was practically everywhere. And because it was lemon season, it seemed a must to sample the town's bounty. It was then and there that I fell for limoncello: lemonade with a kick!

1   Steep together the lemon juice, limoncello, simple syrup, and lemon zest for several hours or overnight. This is your granita base.

2   Add 3 cups (720 ml) water to the granita base and adjust the water/syrup amounts until it tastes the way you want it to.

3   Strain and freeze the granita in a metal baking pan. When it is thoroughly frozen, use a big spoon or fork to scrape it up into icy bits. (The granita can be made several days ahead of time. Before serving, be sure to mix it up thoroughly as the alcohol and sugar will settle to the bottom of your container. A simple stir will distribute everything properly.)

4   Toss sliced strawberries (or fruit of your choice) with a little sugar.

5   Divide the granita among six to eight glasses or bowls. Top each serving with berries and garnish with a few basil leaves. Serve immediately.

HAZELNUT COFFEE MASCARPONE LAYER CAKE

**FOR THE HAZELNUT
GENOISE CAKE:**

3 ounces (85 g) almond paste
1½ cups (300 g) plus
    2 tablespoons sugar
6 large eggs
4 egg yolks
1 teaspoon orange zest
½ teaspoon vanilla extract
¼ teaspoon almond extract
1 cup plus 2 tablespoons
    (135 g) cake flour
¼ teaspoon salt
1 cup (115 g) hazelnut flour
½ cup (120 ml) clarified
    butter (see Note on page
    298)

FOR THE GANACHE:

8 ounces (225 g) bittersweet
    chocolate
1¼ cups (300 ml) heavy
    cream
Pinch of salt
ingredients continue

Here is a wonderful Heather Miller creation. Heather knows about my chocolate sweet tooth, and she also understands my lust for espresso. Coupled with hazelnuts and a bit of orange zest, this cake makes a terrific end to any meal. Proper genoise is a good lesson in cookery. All home cooks should aspire to have this Italian sponge cake under their belts. It is not an easy get however; if at first you fail, please do not give up. Patience and the extra effort will pay off.

1   Make the hazelnut genoise cake: Preheat the oven to 375°F (190°C). Grease a half sheet pan and line it with parchment paper. Bring a small pot of water to a boil.

2   In a stand mixer fitted with the paddle attachment, beat the almond paste and very slowly mix in 1½ cups (300 g) of the sugar, the eggs, and the yolks, stopping and scraping the sides of the bowl often to make sure there are no almond paste lumps. Add the orange zest.

3   When the sugar and eggs are fully incorporated, remove the bowl from the mixer and whisk over the boiling water until warm to the touch. *recipe continues*

FOR THE COFFEE MASCARPONE:

1 cup (240 g) mascarpone
3 tablespoons sugar, plus more
    to taste
2 cups (480 ml) heavy cream
½ teaspoon vanilla extract
2 teaspoons coffee extract, or
    more to taste
Pinch of salt

FOR THE VANILLA SYRUP:

½ cup (100 g) sugar
1 teaspoon vanilla extract

FOR THE CARAMELIZED HAZELNUTS:

1 cup (135 g) toasted
    hazelnuts, loosened skins
    rubbed off
1 cup (200 g) sugar

TO SERVE:

2 tablespoons cocoa nibs or
    cocoa powder for garnish

*Note: To make clarified butter,
microwave for 2 minutes on
high in a glass bowl, then
skim off the cream.*

4   Return the bowl to the mixer, switch to the whip attachment, and whip on medium-high speed until the mixture is very thick and pale. Mix in the vanilla and almond extracts. Remove the bowl from the mixer, transfer the contents to a big mixing bowl, and sift in the flour, the remaining 2 tablespoons sugar, and the salt, gently folding in the dry ingredients. Fold in the hazelnut flour.

5   In a separate bowl, combine about 1 cup (240 ml) of the batter with the clarified butter, mixing gently but thoroughly, and then add to the rest of the batter and mix to combine. Pour the batter into the prepared sheet pan. Bake for 12 to 14 minutes, until the cake springs back when touched in the center. Let the cake cool completely, then turn it out of the pan.

6   Make the ganache: Chop the chocolate into tiny pieces.

7   Heat the cream in a small saucepan until hot but not boiling and pour it over the chocolate. Whisk until the chocolate is melted, then add salt to taste. Let the ganache cool until it is thick enough to spread. If it gets too thick, heat it up a little over a pot of boiling water, whisking until it thins out.

8   Make the coffee mascarpone: Put the mascarpone and sugar in the bowl of a stand mixer with the whip attachment. Add about ½ cup (120 ml) of the cream and whip on medium-low speed until no lumps of mascarpone remain.

9   Add the remaining 1½ cups (360 ml) cream, the vanilla and coffee extracts, and the pinch of salt and whip just until thick and spreadable. Do not overwhip or your cream will become grainy and greasy-tasting. Taste and add more coffee extract if needed.

10   Make the vanilla syrup: In a small saucepan, bring ½ cup (120 ml) water and the sugar to a boil. Remove from the heat, cool to room temperature, and stir in the vanilla.

11   Make the caramelized hazelnuts: Place the hazelnuts on a sheet pan lined with parchment paper.

12 Put the sugar in a tall-sided pot and add just enough water to make it wet, plus a little more, about ¼ cup (60 ml) total. Be very careful not to get any sugar on the sides of the pot. Cover the pot and cook over low heat until the sugar syrup comes to a boil. Turn up the heat and let the syrup boil for 1 to 2 minutes with the lid on, so the steam will wash away any sugar that might be on the sides of the pot.

13 Remove the lid and let it boil over high heat until the sugar starts to caramelize and brown. Don't stir! (Stirring will cause the sugar to crystallize.) Watch the sugar syrup closely as it boils. When the syrup starts to brown, swirl it around in the pot so it browns more uniformly, but don't stir. When it reaches a dark golden brown, after 3 to 5 minutes of boiling, very carefully pour it over the hazelnuts to coat them and leave to cool.

14 When the nuts have cooled completely, chop them in a food processor or by hand into small pieces. Don't do this on a humid day or you will have a sticky mess instead of crunchy caramel.

15 Assemble the cake: Use a long serrated knife to trim the edges of the cake, then cut the cake crosswise into thirds to make three rectangles.

16 Place one rectangle of cake on a serving platter and sprinkle one-third of the vanilla syrup over it to moisten it. Spread a thin layer of ganache over the cake, then a layer of coffee mascarpone cream, and then top with a second layer of cake. Sprinkle with syrup, then spread with ganache, then with coffee cream. Repeat with the third cake layer, finishing with coffee cream.

17 Cover the cake with plastic wrap and chill in the refrigerator until it is set, about 4 hours.

18 To serve, cut into slices and sprinkle with the caramelized hazelnuts and cocoa nibs or cocoa powder.

CANNOLIS

FOR THE PASTRIES:

2 cups plus 2 tablespoons
(255 g) all-purpose flour
1 tablespoon plus
1½ teaspoons sugar
¼ teaspoon salt
½ cup (120 ml) red wine, or
more if needed
Oil for deep-frying

FOR THE RICOTTA:

2 cups (480 ml) milk
½ cup (120 ml) heavy cream
1 tablespoon lemon juice or
champagne vinegar
¼ teaspoon salt

FOR THE FILLING:

¾ cup (180 ml) heavy cream
3 tablespoons (35 g) sugar
¼ cup plus 2 tablespoons
(90 ml) whole milk
1½ teaspoons powdered
gelatin
2 yolks
½ teaspoon vanilla
Pinch of salt

Cannolis are the essence of Italian desserts. They embody the great traditions of Italian pastry history, and they are a great crowd pleaser. The use of red wine ensures a Barbuto touch. Heather Miller concocted this version to keep our customers on their toes. The red wine not only adds flavor but also makes the cannoli dough crisper and adds a deeper color. The filling, adapted from a ricotta Bavarian recipe by Richard Sax, in his *Classic Home Desserts*, really is sublime.

1   Make the pastries: Mix together the flour, sugar, and salt in the bowl of a stand mixer.

2   Add the wine and mix with a dough hook until a smooth dough is formed. It may take a little more wine, but don't make the dough too wet.

3   Let the dough rest for at least 2 hours.

4   Roll out the dough in a pasta machine to #7. Cut dough into roughly 4 × 2½-inch rectangles. Wrap each rectangle around a cannoli tube, gluing the overlapping ends together with a little water, then put in the freezer for 5 to 10 minutes.

5   Heat the oil to 375°F (190°C). Fry the pastries until golden. They will continue to cook a little after they come out of the oil, so don't let them get too dark.

6   Make the filling: Line a small colander with cheesecloth that has been washed in hot water and wrung dry. Place the colander in a bowl. *recipe continues*

7   Make the ricotta: Heat the milk and cream in a ceramic saucepan until simmering. Remove from heat and add the lemon juice and salt.

8   Stir gently until the mixture forms curds. Immediately place the contents of the saucepan into the cheesecloth. Allow to set up until firm and cool. Makes about 1 cup ricotta.

9   Transfer the cooled ricotta to a medium mixing bowl. Stir vigorously to remove any lumps. Set aside.

10   In a medium bowl, using a handheld mixer (or in the bowl of a stand mixer), whip the heavy cream until soft peaks form.

11   Put 2 tablespoons of the milk in another bowl and sprinkle the gelatin on top. Set aside for a few minutes to allow the gelatin time to rehydrate.

12   In a small saucepan over medium heat, heat the remaining milk.

13   In a small bowl, beat the egg yolks with 3 tablespoons sugar, then slowly whisk in the warm milk. Return the mixture to the saucepan and cook, stirring constantly, over low heat until the mixture thickens slightly and coats the back of a spoon.

14   Remove from the heat, and while the sauce is still warm, stir in the gelatin and vanilla extract. Strain through a fine-mesh strainer into a bowl.

15   Allow to cool, stirring so it doesn't get lumpy or rubbery.

16   When cool but not cold, place in a stainless-steel bowl. Whisk in the ricotta, then fold in the whipped cream. Taste and add more salt and vanilla if desired. Chill until set. This is your basic cannoli filling—add chopped chocolate, orange zest, whatever your heart desires!

17   Pipe the filling into the cannolis and then dust with confectioner's sugar.

CARAMEL PANNA COTTA

SERVES 4

½ cup (100 g) sugar
1 cup (240 ml) heavy cream
1 cup (240 ml) milk
2 teaspoons powdered gelatin
¼ teaspoon salt
1 teaspoon vanilla extract

Panna cotta is a very special dessert that is a great introduction to pastry making. It has all the elements one needs to create wonderful desserts: You will make a caramel sauce and finally a frozen concoction that will wow everyone. *Panna* means cream, and *cotta* is the process of freezing. I find this recipe to be universal; you can substitute the caramel with chocolate, fruit puree, or butterscotch.

1   In a heavy copper or stainless-steel pan, cook the sugar to a dark caramel color—do not stir! Put the sugar in a tall-sided pot and add just enough water to make it wet, plus a little more, about ¼ cup (60 ml) total. Be very careful not to get any sugar on the sides of the pot. Cover the pot and cook over low heat until the sugar syrup comes to a boil. Turn up the heat and let the syrup boil for 1 to 2 minutes with the lid on, so the steam will wash away any sugar that might be on the sides of the pot.

2   Remove the lid and let it boil over high heat until the sugar starts to caramelize and brown. Don't stir! (Stirring will cause the sugar to crystallize.) Watch the sugar syrup closely as it boils. When the syrup starts to brown, swirl it around in the pot so it browns more uniformly, but don't stir.

3   While the sugar is caramelizing, sprinkle the gelatin over the milk.

4   When the sugar reaches the desired color, turn down the heat to low and very slowly add the cream. Be careful, as the mixture may splatter. When all the cream has been added and the caramel has dissolved, whisk in the milk/gelatin mixture.

5   Strain, add salt and vanilla and chill until it just starts to thicken. Pour into molds and chill overnight.

AFFOGATO

FOR THE VANILLA GELATO:

1 cup (240 ml) heavy cream
1 cup (240 ml) milk
1 vanilla bean
4 egg yolks
⅓ cup (65 g) sugar
Pinch of sea salt
¼ teaspoon vanilla extract, or
   to taste

TO SERVE:

3 ounces hot brewed espresso

When it comes time for the final roundup, affogato plus some budino is the way to go! A perfectly crafted double espresso poured over a densely flavored vanilla bean ice cream—now that is heaven.

1   Make the vanilla gelato: In a heavy saucepan, heat the cream, milk, and vanilla bean (sliced in half and the seeds scraped into the liquid) until very hot but not boiling. Remove from the heat and let sit for 1 hour or so.

2   When you are ready, reheat the liquid until it is very hot. Remove the vanilla bean pod.

3   Whisk together the egg yolks and sugar in a bowl and slowly add the hot liquid, whisking constantly. Return to the pan and cook, stirring constantly, until the mixture thickens slightly and coats the back of a spoon. Remove from the heat, strain, and chill overnight.

4   The next day, stir in a little salt and vanilla extract to taste, and then freeze according to your ice cream maker's instructions. Freeze overnight in your freezer.

5   To serve: Next dinner, scoop a nice 3-ounce (90 ml) ball of ice cream into an amaro glass, make an espresso, and pour on top. Heaven.

ACKNOWLEDGMENTS

I would like to thank my Barbuto customers. I tried to build something different, a joint that is as comfortable as your favorite shoe, as rich as your best relationship, and as fun as watching puppies romp.

The word "restaurant" comes from the French and means literally to restore one's spirit. In that regard, I hope this book will serve the same purpose, to give everyone a little of that energy and spirit you all inject into Barbuto.

For the sourcing of ingredients, I offer a genuine thanks to the farmers, butchers, fishermen, cheesemongers, and other amazing suppliers. These invaluable people are the cornerstone of my food and are surely the reason why so many people just love Barbuto. The hidden figures, the perpetual-motion people who pick up the garbage, deliver the linen, and clean the exhaust system—thankless jobs, but totally appreciated. Of course, my managers, cooks, chefs, waiters, bussers, runners, hosts, and prep cooks, and my unsung heroes, the dishwashers.

Barbuto is truly a family, a community, a safe haven. It started from a desire of my partner, Fabrizio Ferri, to have a restaurant in the ground floor of his photography and event business, Industria Superstudio. The Barbuto logo is Fabrizio's beautiful and fun portrait of his beloved Gideon, an Irish wolfhound.

My muse in respect to the culinary inspiration for Barbuto is the smart and richly talented Lynn McNeely. Lynn and I have known each other since the mid 1980s. Many, many thanks to my pastry genius, the intrepid and insightful Heather Miller. She is my Rock of Gibraltar, the anchor of the kitchen. Her strengths are many, and she is always the grown-up in the room, constantly questioning her desserts and delicately judging the savory food as well.

I have been fortunate in the chefs who have worked for me, including the effervescent and curious-to-the-point-of-annoyance Justin Smillie. Justin has gone on to greater things, most recently as the chef and creator of Upland, where his starting point of reference was probably Barbuto. There was the inestimable Andrew Curren, who hails from Houston and now lives in Austin, but his email address says it all: "italydrew"!

Two friends of Andrew's, Preston Madson and Ginger Pierce, were part of the original crew. Ginger is now my executive chef at Jams, and Preston, her husband, is also a very creative and competent chef. Kelsie Kerr, a cook who had toiled at Judy Rodgers's Zuni Café and seemed totally at home taming the huge beast of a grill that Nobile Attie and I designed for Barbuto. Roel Alcudia is bright and irreverent, and his fresh take on the Barbuto style drew from his time at Veritas in New York. Hunter Lewis, the current editor of *Food & Wine* magazine, came early on to learn the Barbuto way. He started with a whisper but gradually mastered the seemingly simple intricacies of the line at Barbuto.

"The line," as my cooks refer to our ranges, grill, and ovens, is where the magic happens. One master of the line is a gentleman named Luis Ruiz. His intelligence, speed, and stamina have made him an integral part of the Barbuto landscape. Luis can singlehandedly "run" the line at Barbuto.

Jake Leiber was a youngster when he first staged (i.e., worked a short, introductory stint) at Barbuto. He weathered every summer and then, upon graduation from Wesleyan, announced his intention to stay at Barbuto. He is now the proud chef of his own restaurant. Travis McShane spent his externship at Barbuto and, upon graduation, he returned there. His only culinary jobs were with me, and he rose to become a very trusted, loyal chef and dear friend. Travis is smart and studious, quietly assured, with a real love for the simplicity of Barbuto cooking.

The ongoing list of talented cooks and chefs who have passed through Barbuto runs deep: Jason DeBriere, the chef at Tacombi, and Joel Hough, who would go on to be head chef at Cookshop and Il Buco. The serene and always happy Melissa Lopez ran the kitchen with aplomb. Phillip Basone and Phil Hering will do great things in the future. The quiet and intelligent Ryan Hart now has his own épicerie in Westchester County. Joshua Stumbaugh, a dedicated Barbuto chef, has decamped to Hong Kong to open his own restaurant.

Our dishwashers and prep crew need a standing ovation. A restaurant rests upon a foundation of hardworking individuals, and you are my foundation. I am truly in awe of your work ethic, your cheerfulness, and your loyalty. Thank you, and bravo!

My front-of-the-house team is without parallel. My waitstaff, runners, and bussers are all terrific and sassy, just the way I like it. Some of you have worked for us for a decade or more of amazingly wonderful service.

To the Barbuto bartenders, I know I tortured you with extremely difficult working conditions, but you have turned adversity into success. You made the bar at Barbuto a true gathering spot, no simple task.

To my extremely funny and wickedly smart hosts, you brighten my every day.

My managers are very special people; they form the heart and soul of Barbuto. They tirelessly conquer the myriad challenges that occur on a minute-by-minute basis. Some of these challenges are the intangibles: weather, broken equipment, sick employees, missed deliveries. Carol Gonzalez was my longtime manager and remains a stalwart and enthusiastic Barbuto team member. Above all else is our intention to always treat others with the same respect we claim for ourselves.

The leader of this philosophy is my general manager, Jennifer Davidson. She began as a hostess many years ago, fifteen years to be exact. She is truly a magician with an unusually strong work ethic, and she holds others to this same high standard. Rounding out this team is her counterpart, Michael Kelly. Michael, who was one of my first employees, made the transition from bartender to wine dude to manager. I would not say he always enjoys that role, but he is very good at it. I think Michael would rather be toe-deep in the sand at some faraway beach with a book of poems in his hands. Yet Michael is as committed to Barbuto as Jennifer is, and together they form a strong alliance. This alliance is evident in the happiness of our many satisfied customers. To ensure that thousands of diners a year enjoy a satisfactory Barbuto experience is a near impossible task, really. But Jennifer and Michael seem to hardly sweat; they are the key to my success.

I want to thank my team at CAA. Cait Hoyt, my book agent, did a terrific job of wrangling me and positioning Barbuto as a good idea for a cookbook. She trusted Abrams and its team, and she was correct. And of course, my dear pals at CAA Andrew Chason and Danielle Kim, who allow me to do what I do best, are the ones who always champion and protect me. Daisy Nichols is my tireless, professional, and delightful recipe tester. Her skill with the recipes is surpassed only by her diplomacy in dealing with me.

The team at Abrams, starting with my cool and very smart editor, Michael Sand. Michael is unusually laissez-faire—unless I needed strong editing (often!). He is ever enthusiastic and a stalwart champion of all things Barbuto. He and the other folks at Abrams, Deb Wood in particular, obviously love what they do. They went way over the top to ensure that the photo shoots went well, that the artwork was just so, and that I almost behaved myself! The delicious offices at Abrams highlight what CEO Michael Jacobs thinks of his press. It shows how committed they are to producing special books, worthy of the Abrams imprint.

A special place in the Barbuto realm is held by the partners: Joey Grill, Philip Scotti, Fabrizio Ferri, and Arnold Penner, all of whom I thank for their support over the years.

Lastly, my friends and family, I cannot thank all of you enough. I realize I am a pain the ass; I can be cantankerous, a curmudgeon, and quixotic, and why you all indulge me is a mystery. To my pals Victoria Freeman and Marc Meyer, Jimmy Bradley, Joey Campanaro, Jason Giagrande, and Scott Feldman; all of you have had to endure my nonsense daily. To Michael Weinstein, David Ferber, James Nicholas, Ken Levitan, and Jon Gallen, you have been my faithful advisors. To Aarón Sánchez, thank you for being you. To Sarah Abell, my guardian angel.

A special thanks to my dear friend Jeremy King for his unwavering and extremely patient coddling. To the amazing Schiffers: my beloved, departed friend Craig and his resilient wife, Amy; in sharing their wonderful house in France, they have enabled me to recharge my batteries every summer and forge on.

Finally: heartfelt thanks to my sons, Foster and Alexander, and my daughter, Hannah. And to the ever-effervescent Sally, you are and always will be the inspiration for Barbuto.

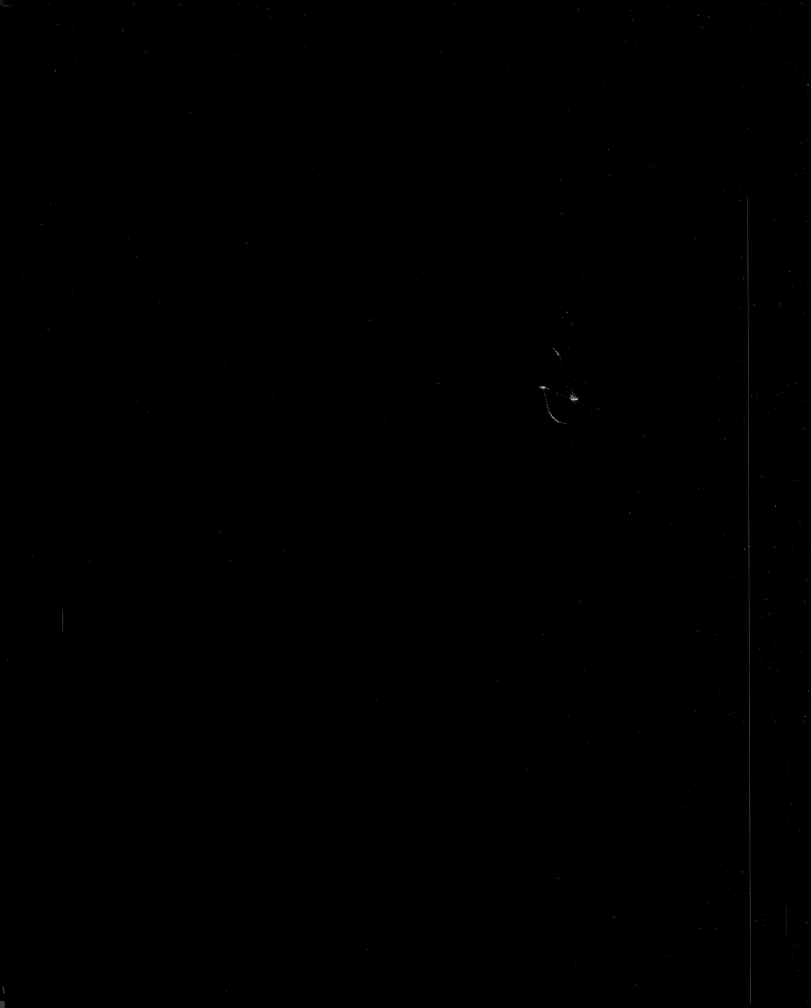

INDEX

Adele's, 287
Affogato, 304, *305*
aioli
    Aioli, 249
    Paprika Aioli, 231
Alcudia, Roel, 20
all'amatriciana, 155, *156*
Almodóvar, Pedro, 9
Amatriciana, 156, *157*
anchovies, 174–75, *175*
    Anchovy Butter, 244
    Anchovy Vinaigrette, *96*, 97
Andrews, Colman, 87
antipasti, 48–49. *See also* bruschetta;
    soup
    Asparagus and Prosciutto, 74
    Beef Carpaccio and Truffles,
        76–77
    Breadsticks, 88–90, *89*
    Crespelle With Chestnut Honey,
        72–73, *73*
    Fonduta, 91
    Porcini and Garlic, 86
    Rosemary Focaccia, 84, *85*
    Socca!, 87
    Sole Crudo, *60*, 61
    Squash Blossoms, 78–79
    Zucchini Caviar, 75
Apricot Charlotte, *292, 293*
Aqua Fresca, *256*, 257
Arborio rice, 121, 152, 184
Arrington, Nyesha, 10
arugula, 222, *223*
asparagus
    Asparagus and Prosciutto, 74

Asparagus Pizza, *40*, 41
Gnocchi with Asparagus and
    Morels, 145
Shaved Veg Salad, 114, *115*
Attie, Nobile, 17–18, 28–29, 191,
    202–3
autumn vegetables, 56–57
avocado, 61, 99, 108–9

Baby Gem Salad, 99
bacon, 36, 119, 147, 197, 210
Baked Hake, 178, *179*
Balazs, André, 14
Balsamic vinegar, 88–90
Bank Street Buck, *256*, 257
Barbuto, 8–11, 24
    business model of, 16–17
    history of, 13–15
    menu of, 20–21
Barbuto Potatoes, 240, *241*
basil. *See also* pesto
    Basil Oil, 59, 251
    Pizza Bambini, 37
bass, 174–75, *175*, 184
Bastianich, Lidia, 15
beef
    Beef Carpaccio and Truffles,
        76–77, 82–83
    Hanger Steak with Salsa Picante,
        209
    Oxtail Soup, 56–57
    Pasta Bolognese, *146*, 147
    Skirt Steak Romesco, 203
beets, 236, *237*

berries
    Limoncello Granita with Berries,
        294, 295
    Peach and Blueberry Crostatas,
        264–66, *265*
    Shortcake with Berries, 271
    Strawberry Layer Cake, *286*,
        287–88
    Strawberry Pavlovas, *268*, 269
Bianco, Chris, 70
Biga, 31
Biscotti, *261, 263*
Black Truffle Pizza, 45
blood oranges, *60*, 61
blueberries
    Peach and Blueberry Crostatas,
        264–66, *265*
Blue Crab Bruschetta, 68
boar, 136–37. *See also* pork
de Boer, Clare, 8
Bourdain, Anthony, 10
bread. *See also* bruschetta
    Breadsticks, 88–90, *89*
    ciabatta, 51
    croutons, 62, *63*, 64
    Heirloom Panzanella, 105
    Rosemary Focaccia, 84, *85*
broccoli
    broccolini, 174–75, *175*
    broccoli rabe, 139–40
    Pasta, Sausage, and Broccoli di
        Ciccio, 133
    spigarello, 219
Broiled Char with Chanterelles,
    181–82

broth, vegetable, 53
brown butter, 174–75, *175*, *278*, 279–81
bruschetta, 65–71
    Blue Crab Bruschetta, 68
    Fontina and Ramp Bruschetta, 71
    Peas and Ricotta Bruschetta, 66, *67*
    Tuna Tonnato Bruschetta, 70
    Wild Mushrooms, Ricotta, and Parsley Bruschetta, 69
Brussels sprouts
    Brussels Sprout Pizza, 42, *43*
    Brussels Sprouts Barbuto, *242*, 243
    Brussels Sprouts Salad, *100*, 101
bucatini
    Bucatini All'Amatriciana, 156, *157*
    Bucatini with Pesto, 119
Budino, 272–73
butter
    Anchovy Butter, 244
    brown butter, 174–75, *175*, *278*, 279–81
    Chocolate-Brown Butter Tart, *278*, 279–81
    Mint Butter, 206–8, *207*
butternut squash, 51

Caesar Salad, 110–11
cake
    Coconut-Nut Teacakes, 285
    Genoise Cake, 274, 287, 296
    Hazelnut Coffee Mascarpone Layer Cake, 296–99, *297*
    Lemon-Pistachio Cake, 274–76, *275*
    Shortcake with Berries, 271
    Strawberry Layer Cake, *286*, *287–88*
    Tiramisu, 290, *291*
Calamari Salad, 106, *107*
California Cuisine, 7–8
Campanaro, Joey, 82
Cannolis, 300–302, *301*
Capesante, 180
Caramel Ice Cream, 277

Caramel Panna Cotta, 303
Carbonara, 122–23
cardoons, 220–21
Carenno, Carolynn, 110
carne, 202. *See also specific types*
carrots, 52–53, 56–57, 59, 229
    Shaved Veg Salad, 114, *115*
Castelvetrano olives, 104
cauliflower
    Cauliflower Soufflé, 238
    Cauliflower Soup, 58
celery, 114
Chambrette, Ferdinand, 72
chanterelles, 39, 45, 69
    Broiled Char with Chanterelles, 181–82
char, 181–82
Chase, Leah, 10
cheese. *See also* mascarpone; ricotta
    farmer's cheese, 236, *237*
    fontina, 32, 71, 91
    goat cheese, *40*, 41
    Gruyère cheese, 39, 83, 91, 239
    mozzarella, 36, 37, 44
    Parmesan, 34, 88–90, *89*
    Pecorino Romano, *96*, 97–98, *126*, 127, 230
    Roquefort cheese, 238
Chenin Blanc, 120
Chestnut Honey, 72–73, *73*
Chez Panisse, 29, 160, 195
chicken, 29
    Chicken Livers, 62, *63*, 64
    Chicken Richard Olney, 198–99
    Chicken Soup, 59
    JW Chicken, *190*, 191–93, *192*, *193*
Child, Julia, 267
chiles
    Calabrian chiles, 250
    Fresno chiles, *55*, *60*, 61, 152, 250
    Hatch chiles, 218
    Poblano chiles, 234
chocolate
    Budino, 272–73
    Chocolate-Brown Butter Tart, *278*, 279–81

Chocolate Meringue Cookies, 289
    Chocolate Shortbread, 282, *283*
    Ganache, 296–98, *297*
    Gianduja Soufflé, 267
    Milk Chocolate Spritz, 284
chorizo sausage
    Chorizo and Kale Pizza, 44
    Pasta, Sausage, and Broccoli di Ciccio, 133
    Spanish chorizo, 184
ciabatta, 51, 105, 293
Cioppino, 164–66, *165*
citrus, 219
    blood orange, *60*, 61
    Citrus Salad, 104
    Lemon Pasta, 150
    Lemon-Pistachio Cake, 274–76, *275*
    Meyer lemon, 108–9, 111, 150
clams
    Cioppino, 164–66, *165*
    Clam Linguini, *128*, 129
    Clam Pizza, 34
cocktails, *253*
    Aqua Fresca, *256*, 257
    Bank Street Buck, *256*, 257
    Dr. McConack's Magical Tonic, 254, *255*
    The Fennel Countdown, 258, *259*
    JW Margarita, 254, *255*
    Negroni Cativo, *256*, 257
    1919, 254, *255*
    Paloma Milano, 258, *259*
    The Poppet, *256*, 257
    Rosé Sangria, 254, *255*
    Tempestoso, 258, *259*
Coconut-Nut Teacakes, 285
cod, *176*, 177
coffee
    Coffee Mascarpone, 298
    Tiramisu, 290, *291*
Collard Greens and Farro, 151–52
condiments. *See* sauces and condiments
cookies
    Biscotti, *261*, 263, *263*
    Chocolate Meringue Cookies, 289

Chocolate Shortbread, 282, *283*
Coconut-Nut Teacakes, 285
Milk Chocolate Spritz, 284
corn, 180
    Corn and Tomato Gnocchi,
        142–44, *143*
    Pan-Roasted Tilefish, 167
    Succotash, 234–35
cranberry beans, 180, 234–35
cream, 210–11
crème fraîche, 45
crepes, 72–73, *73*
Crespelle With Chestnut Honey,
    72–73, *73*
cress, 62, *63*, 64
crostatas, 264, *265*
croutons, 62, *63*, 64
cucumber, *170*, 171
Curren, Andrew, 20

dairy. *See also* butter; ice cream
    cream, 210–11
    crème fraîche, 45
Davidson, Jen, 20
Delicata Gnocchi, *138*, 139–40
desserts. *See also* cookies; ice cream
    Apricot Charlotte, *292*, 293
    Budino, 272–73
    Cannolis, 300–302, *301*
    Caramel Panna Cotta, 303
    Chocolate-Brown Butter Tart,
        278, 279–81
    Gianduja Soufflé, 267
    Hazelnut Coffee Mascarpone
        Layer Cake, 296–99, *297*
    Lemon-Pistachio Cake, 274–76,
        275
    Peach and Blueberry Crostatas,
        264–66, *265*
    Shortcake with Berries, 271
    Strawberry Layer Cake, *286*,
        287–88
    Strawberry Pavlovas, *268*, 269
    Tiramisu, 290, *291*
dressings, 99
Dr. McConack's Magical Tonic,
    254, *255*

duck
    Duck, Peas, and Morels, *194*,
        195–96
    Duck Breast, 197

edamame, 150, 167, 234–35
eggplant
    Eggplant Pizza, 35
    Ratatouille, 246–47
eggs
    Gianduja Soufflé, 267
    Meringue, 270
    Pizza Uovo, 32, *33*
    Pork Chop Milanese al Uovo,
        210–11

farmer's cheese, 236, *237*
farmer's market, 10, 78, 160, 229,
    287,
farro, 151–52
fennel, *54*, 55, 151, 229, *229*
    The Fennel Countdown, 258, *259*
    Fennel Salt, 258
Ferri, Fabrizio, 15, 48, 88
fish and seafood, 159–61
    anchovies, 174–75, *175*
    Anchovy Vinaigrette, *96*, 97
    Baked Hake, 178, *179*
    Blue Crab Bruschetta, 68
    Broiled Char with Chanterelles,
        181–82
    Calamari Salad, 106, *107*
    Capesante, 180
    Cioppino, 164–66, *165*
    Clam Linguini, *128*, 129
    Clam Pizza, 34
    Grilled Soft-Shell Crabs, *168*, 169
    Little Fish Risotto, 120–21
    mussels, *54*, 55, 164–66, *165*
    Pan-Roasted Tilefish, 167
    Parchment-Baked Cod, *176*, 177
    Plancha Shrimp, *80*, 81
    Red Snapper, 172, *173*
    Rock Shrimp Pasta, *148*, 149
    Sally's Birthday Paella, 184
    Shrimp Risotto, 152
    Sole Crudo, *60*, 61

    Striped Bass Steak, 174–75, *175*
    Swordfish with Tomato-
        Cucumber Salsa, *170*, 171
    Trout with Toasted Hazelnuts,
        183
    Tuna Tonnato Bruschetta, 70
    Whole Sea Bream, *159*, 162–63
    Whole Steelhead, 185
    Zuppa di Cozze, *54*, 55
Fisherman's Stew. *See* Cioppino
Flay, Bobby, 8
focaccia, 84, *85*
Fonduta, 91
fontina, 32, 91
    Fontina and Ramp Bruschetta, 71
Food Network, 7
Food & Wine (magazine), 120
fregola, *54*, 55
Fresh Pasta Dough, 137
Fresno chiles, *60*, 61
Frisée, Radicchio, and Pear Salad,
    113
fruit. *See also* berries; citrus
    Apricot Charlotte, *292*, 293
    Melon and Prosciutto Salad, 102,
        103
    Peach and Blueberry Crostatas,
        264–66, *265*
    pear, 62, *63*, 64, 113
    Watermelon Juice, 257

Ganache, 296–98, *297*
Gatto Nero, 120
gelato, 304, *305*
Genoise Cake, 274, 287, 296
Gianduja Soufflé, 267
Giglio, Anthony, 70
Ginger Syrup, 258
Giovanni's Pizzeria, 28
Girardet, 277
gnocchi, *141*
    Corn and Tomato Gnocchi,
        142–44, *143*
    Delicata Gnocchi, *138*, 139–40
    Gnocchi with Asparagus and
        Morels, 145
goat cheese, *40*, 41

Gold, Jonathan, 10
grains
    Arborio rice, 121, 152, 184
    farro, 151–52
    polenta, 82–83
Green Goddess Dressing, 99
Grilled Soft-Shell Crabs, *168*, 169
grisini, 88–90, *89*
Gruyère cheese, 39, 83, 91, 239
guanciale, 156, *157*
Guérard, Michel, 62

hake fillets, 178, *179*
hanger steak
    Hanger Steak and Arugula, 222,
        223
    Hanger Steak with Salsa Picante,
        209
Harry's Bar, 15–16
Hatch chiles, 218
hazelnut
    Hazelnut Coffee Mascarpone
        Layer Cake, 296–99, *297*
    Hazelnut Pesto, 251
    Trout with Toasted Hazelnuts, 183
    Wilted Chard and Hazelnuts,
        232, *233*
Heirloom Panzanella, 105
Heirloom Tomato Salsa, 249
Henderson, Fergus, 212
herbs, 153, *154*
    basil, 37, 59, 251
    chives, 180
    mint, 114, 206–8, *207*, 251
    parsley, 35, 69, 151–52
    rosemary, *84*, 85, 257
    Zucchini and Herb Stuffing,
        198–99
the High Line, 14
honey
    Chestnut Honey, 72–73, *73*
    Turmeric Honey, 254

ice cream
    Affogato, 304
    Caramel Ice Cream, 277
Israeli couscous, *54*, 55

Italian My Way (Waxman, J.), 30,
    272, 290
Italy, 15–16

Jeanty, Philippe, 136
Jerusalem Artichoke Soup, 52–53
JW Chicken, *190*, 191–93, *192*, *193*
JW Margarita, 254, *255*

Kahan, Paul, 219
kale, 51, 230
    Chorizo and Kale Pizza, 44
    Kale Salad, *96*, 97–98
Keller, Thomas, 8
Kelly, Michael, 20

lamb
    Lamb Chops with Mint Butter,
        206–8, *207*
    Leg of Lamb, 215
    St. John Lamb, 212–13, *214*
leeks, 51, 151
Leg of Lamb, 215
legumes
    cranberry beans, 180, 234–35
    edamame, 150, 167, 234–35
    lentils, 172, *173*
    yellow beans, 59
lemon, 219
    Lemon Pasta, 150
    Lemon-Pistachio Cake, 274–76,
        275
    Lemon Simple Syrup, 295
    Limoncello Granita with Berries,
        294, 295
    Meyer lemon, 108–9, 111, 150
lentils, 172, *173*
Lewis, Hunter, 120
Limoncello Granita with Berries,
    294, 295
linguine, 129
Little Fish Risotto, 120–21
Lombardi's, 28
Lopez, Melissa, 20, 97

Maine lobster, 184
margarita, 254, *255*

mascarpone
    Hazelnut Coffee Mascarpone
        Layer Cake, 296–99, *297*
    Lemon-Mascarpone Cream,
        274–76, *275*
    Mascarpone Cream, *286*, 287–88
    Tiramisu, 290, *291*
Mashed Potatoes, 227
May, Tony, 15
McEnroe, John, 7
McNeely, Lynn, 14, 17, 20
McShane, Travis, 20
meat, 202. *See also specific types*
Meatballs and Polenta, 82–83
Melon and Prosciutto Salad, 102,
    103
meringue, 289
Meyer lemon, 108–9, 111, 150
Michael's, 62, 127, 197, 267
Milk Chocolate Spritz, 284
Miller, Heather, 20, 85, 262, 274,
    296
mint, 114
    Mint Butter, 206–8, *207*
    Mint Pesto, 251
Mint Butter, 206–8, *207*
morels
    Duck, Peas, and Morels, *194*,
        195–96
    Gnocchi with Asparagus and
        Morels, 145
mostarda
    Mostarda, *204*, 205, 249
    Pear Mostarda, 62, *63*, 64
Moullé, Jean-Pierre, 195
mozzarella
    Chorizo and Kale Pizza, 44
    Pizza Bambini, 37
    Sweet Potato Pizza, 36
mushrooms
    Beef Carpaccio and Truffles,
        76–77
    Black Truffle Pizza, 45
    Broiled Char with Chanterelles,
        181–82
    Duck, Peas, and Morels, *194*,
        195–96

Gnocchi with Asparagus and Morels, 145
Porcini and Garlic, 86
White Truffle Ravioli, 134–35
Wild Mushroom Pizza, *38*, 39
Wild Mushrooms, Ricotta, and Parsley Bruschetta, 69
mussels, *54*, 55, 164–66, *165*

Negroni Cativo, *256*, 257
New York Times (newspaper), 17
1919 cocktail, 254, *255*
nuts. *See also* hazelnut
Coconut-Nut Teacakes, 285
Lemon-Pistachio Cake, 274–76, *275*
pepitas, 139
pistachios, *60*, 61, 236, *237*, 274–76, *275*

oil, 59, 251. *See also* sauces and condiments
olives, 75, 104
Olive Tapenade, *159*, 162–63
Olney, Richard, 198
oranges, blood, *60*, 61, 104
ovens, 17, 20, 29, 202
Oxtail Soup, 56–57

paella, 184
Paloma Milano, 258, *259*
pancakes, 88
pancetta, 32, *33*, 36
panna cotta, 303
Pan-Roasted Tilefish, 167
Pan-Roasted Vegetables, *228*, 229
panzanella, 105
Paprika Aioli, 231
Parchment-Baked Cod, *176*, 177
Parmesan, 34, 88–90, *89*
parsley, 35, 69, 120–21, 151
Passion Fruit Syrup, 254, 258
pasta
Bucatini All'Amatriciana, 156, *157*
Bucatini with Pesto, 119
Clam Linguini, *128*, 129

Corn and Tomato Gnocchi, 142–44, *143*
Delicata Gnocchi, *138*, 139–40
fregola, *54*, 55
Fresh Pasta Dough, 137
Gnocchi with Asparagus and Morels, 145
Lemon Pasta, 150
Pasta, Sausage, and Broccoli di Ciccio, 133
Pasta Bolognese, *146*, 147
Pasta Cacio e Pepe, *126*, 127
Pasta Carbonara, 122–23
Pasta Pomodoro, 130, *131*, 132
Rock Shrimp Pasta, *148*, 149
spaetzle, 56–57
Spare Rib Ragù Pasta, 155
White Truffle Ravioli, 134–35
Wild Boar Pasta, 136–37
pastries, 260–62. *See also* cookies; desserts
Peach and Blueberry Crostatas, 264–66, *265*
pear
Frisée, Radicchio, and Pear Salad, 113
Pear Mostarda, 62, *63*, 64
peas, 52–53, 59
Duck, Peas, and Morels, *194*, 195–96
Peas and Ricotta Bruschetta, 66, *67*
Pecorino Romano, *96*, 97–98, *126*, 127, 230
Peel, Mark, 62
Pépin, Jacques, 7
pepitas, 139
pesto, 145
Bucatini with Pesto, 119
Hazelnut Pesto, 251
Mint Pesto, 251
Winter Pesto, 251
pistachios, *60*, 61, 236, *237*
Lemon-Pistachio Cake, 274–76, *275*
pizza, 28–29
Asparagus Pizza, *40*, 41
Biga, 31

Black Truffle Pizza, 45
Brussels Sprout Pizza, 42, *43*
Chorizo and Kale Pizza, 44
Clam Pizza, 34
Eggplant Pizza, 35
ovens, 17, 20, 29
Pizza Bambini, 37
Pizza Dough, 30–31, *31*
Pizza Uovo, 32, *33*
Sweet Potato Pizza, 36
Wild Mushroom Pizza, *38*, 39
Plancha Shrimp, *80*, 81
polenta, 82–83
The Poppet, *256*, 257
Porchetta, 216–17
Porcini and Garlic, 86
pork, 48, 82–83
Asparagus and Prosciutto, 74
bacon, 36, 119, 147, 197, 210
Chorizo and Kale Pizza, 44
Melon and Prosciutto Salad, 102, *103*
pancetta, 32, *33*, 36
Pasta, Sausage, and Broccoli di Ciccio, 133
Pasta Bolognese, *146*, 147
Porchetta, 216–17
Pork Chop Milanese al Uovo, 210–11
Pork Chops and Mostarda, *204*, 205
Pork Stew, 218
prosciutto, *40*, 41, 74, 102, *103*
Sausage Ragù Pasta, 153, *154*
Spare Rib Ragù Pasta, 155
Wild Boar Pasta, 136–37
potatoes, 34. *See also* gnocchi
Barbuto Potatoes, 240, *241*
Fingerling, 34
Mashed Potatoes, 227
Russet, 140, 240
Sweet Potato Pizza, 36
Yukon Gold, 227, 229
poultry, 188–89. *See also* chicken; duck
prosciutto
Asparagus and Prosciutto, 74

prosciutto *continued*
    Asparagus Pizza, *40*, 41
    Melon and Prosciutto Salad, 102, *103*
Puck, Wolfgang, 29
pudding
    Apricot Charlotte, *292*, 293
    Budino, 272–73
Puget Sound mussels, 166

radicchio, 113
radishes, 59, 114, 197
ragù
    Ragù, 136–37
    Sausage Ragù Pasta, 153
    Spare Rib Ragù Pasta, *154*, 155
ramps, 128–29, *194*, 195–96
    Fontina and Ramp Bruschetta, 71
Ratatouille, 246–47
ravioli, 134–35
Red Goddess Salad, 108–9
Red Rooster, 9
red snapper, 162–63
    Red Snapper, 172, *173*
Reichl, Ruth, 8, 86
Rib-Eye Steak, 219
Ribollita, *50*, 51
ricotta
    Eggplant Pizza, 35
    Peas and Ricotta Bruschetta, 66, *67*
    Pizza Uovo, 32, *33*
    Sausage Ragù Pasta, 153, *154*
    Wild Mushrooms, Ricotta, and Parsley Bruschetta, 69
risotto
    Little Fish Risotto, 120–21
    Shrimp Risotto, 152
Roasted Beets, 236, *237*
Roasted Romanesco, 239
Roasted Turnips, 244, *245*
Rock Shrimp Pasta, *148*, 149
romanesco, 239
romesco
    Romesco Salsa, 203, 250
    Skirt Steak Romesco, 203

Roquefort cheese, 238
rosemary
    Rosemary Focaccia, 84, *85*
    Rosemary Syrup, 257
Rosé Sangria, 254, *255*
rosé wine, 106
Ruiz, Luis, 9, 130, 132

saffron, 120–21, 166, 184
salad, 94–95
    Baby Gem Salad, 99
    Brussels Sprouts Salad, *100*, 101
    Caesar Salad, 110–11
    Calamari Salad, 106, *107*
    Citrus Salad, 104
    Frisée, Radicchio, and Pear Salad, 113
    Heirloom Panzanella, 105
    Kale Salad, *96*, 97–98
    Melon and Prosciutto Salad, 102, *103*
    Red Goddess Salad, 108–9
Sally's Birthday Paella, 184
salsas
    Heirloom Tomato Salsa, 249
    Romesco Salsa, 203, 250
    Salsa Picante, 209, 250
    Salsa Verde, 250
    Tomato-Cucumber Salsa, *170*, 171
salumi, 48
Samuelsson, Marcus, 7–11
Sánchez, Aarón, 8
San Marzano canned tomato, 51, 83, 130–32, 147, 153, 156
sauces and condiments. *See also* salsas
    Aioli, 249
    Anchovy Butter, 244
    Anchovy Vinaigrette, *96*, 97
    Basil Oil, 59, 251
    Bucatini with Pesto, 119
    Fennel Salt, 258
    Ginger Syrup, 258
    Green Goddess Dressing, 99
    Hazelnut Pesto, 251
    Mint Pesto, 251

    Mostarda, *204*, 205, 249
    Olive Tapenade, *159*, 162–63
    Paprika Aioli, 231
    Pasta Bolognese, *146*, 147
    Pear Mostarda, 62, *63*, 64
    ragù, 136–37, 153, *154*, 155
    Rosemary Syrup, 257
    Tomato Sauce, 130, *131*, 132, 249
    Turmeric Honey, 254
    Winter Pesto, 251
sausage
    Chorizo and Kale Pizza, 44
    Pasta, Sausage, and Broccoli di Ciccio, 133
    Sausage Ragù Pasta, 153, *154*
    Spanish chorizo, 184
savory, 56–57
scallions, 197
sea bream, *159*, 162–63
seafood. *See* fish and seafood
sea scallops, 180
Selvaggio, Piero, 15
Shadbolt, Jess, 8
Shaved Veg Salad, 114, *115*
Shi, Annie, 8
Shortbread, 282, *283*
Shortcake with Berries, 271
shrimp, 106, *107*
    Plancha Shrimp, *80*, 81
    Rock Shrimp Pasta, *148*, 149
    Sally's Birthday Paella, 184
    Shrimp Risotto, 152
Silverton, Nancy, 8, 62, 279
Simple French Food (Olney), 198
Skirt Steak Romesco, 203
Smillie, Justin, 8, 20, 216
Socca!, 87
Sole Crudo, *60*, 61
soufflé
    Cauliflower Soufflé, 238
    Gianduja Soufflé, 267
soup, 48–49
    Cauliflower Soup, 58
    Chicken Soup, 59
    Jerusalem Artichoke Soup, 52–53

Oxtail Soup, 56–57
Ribollita, *50*, 51
Vegetable Broth, 53
Zuppa di Cozze, *54*, 55
Spaetzle, 56–57
Spago, 29
Spanish chorizo, 184
Spare Rib Ragù Pasta, 155
spices
    Ginger Syrup, 258
    saffron, 120–21, 166, 184
    Turmeric Honey, 254
spigarello, 219
spinach, 39, 153, *154*, 230
squash
    butternut, 51
    delicata, *138*, 139–40
    Squash Blossoms, 78–79
squid, 106, *107*, 166
Standard Hotel, 14
steak
    Hanger Steak and Arugula, 222, *223*
    Hanger Steak with Salsa Picante, 209
    Rib-Eye Steak, 219
    Skirt Steak Romesco, 203
    Venison steak, 220–21
steelhead, 185
St. John Lamb, 212–13, *214*
strawberries, 295
    Shortcake with Berries, 271
    Strawberry Layer Cake, *286*, 287–88
    Strawberry Pavlovas, *268*, 269
Striped Bass Steak, 174–75, *175*
Stumbaugh, Josh, 20
Succotash, 234–35
sunchokes
    Jerusalem Artichoke Soup, 52–53
    Sunchokes with Paprika Aioli, 231
Sweet Potato Pizza, 36
Swiss chard, 119, 210–11
    Wilted Chard and Hazelnuts, 232, *233*

Swordfish with Tomato-Cucumber Salsa, *170*, 171
syrup
    Ginger Syrup, 258
    Lemon Simple Syrup, 295
    Passion Fruit Syrup, 254, 258
    Rosemary Syrup, 257
    Vanilla Syrup, 276, 287, 298–99

tapenade, olive, *159*, 162–63
tarts
    Chocolate-Brown Butter Tart, *278*, 279–81
    Peach and Blueberry Crostatas, 264–66, *265*
Tempestoso, 258, *259*
Tiramisu, 290, *291*
tomato
    Corn and Tomato Gnocchi, 142–44, *143*
    heirloom, 35, 105, 167, 171, *176*, 177
    Heirloom Panzanella, 105
    Heirloom Tomato Salsa, 249
    Pasta Pomodoro, 130, *131*, *132*
    Romesco Salsa, 203, 250
    San Marzano canned, 51, 83, 130–32, 147, 153, 156
    Sungold, 180
    Tomato-Cucumber Salsa, *170*, 171
    Tomato Sauce, 130, *131*, 132, 249
tonnato, 70
Troisgros, Pierre, 62
trout
    Trout with Toasted Hazelnuts, 183
    Whole Steelhead, 185
truffles. *See also* mushrooms
    Beef Carpaccio and Truffles, 76–77
    Black Truffle Pizza, 45
    White Truffle Ravioli, 134–35
Tuna Tonnato Bruschetta, 70
Turmeric Honey, 254
turnips, *228*, 229, 244, *245*

uovo. *See* eggs
Upland, 216
upland cress, 62, *63*, 64

Vanilla Syrup, 276, 287, 298–99
veal, 82–83, *146*, 147
vegetables, 226. *See also specific vegetables*
    Vegetable Broth, 53
Venison with Braised Cardoons, 220–21
Vergé, Roger, 62
Vincente, Mauro, 15, 127

Washington Park, 9, 14
Watermelon Juice, 257
watermelon radishes, 114
Waters, Alice, 15, 65
Waxman, Alexander, 120–21
Waxman, Jonathan, 30, 272, 290
Waxman, Sally, 16, 120
West Village, 13–14
White Truffle Ravioli, 134–35
Whole Sea Bream, *159*, 162–63
Whole Steelhead, 185
Wild Boar Pasta, 136–37
wild mushrooms. *See also* chanterelle mushrooms; morels
    Porcini and Garlic, 86
    Wild Mushroom Pizza, *38*, 39
    Wild Mushrooms, Ricotta, and Parsley Bruschetta, 69
Williams, Venus, 234
Wilted Chard and Hazelnuts, 232, *233*
wine, 106, 120
Winter Pesto, 251

Yamaguchi, Roy, 62
yellow beans, 59

zucchini
    Ratatouille, 246–47
    Zucchini and Herb Stuffing, 198–99
    Zucchini Caviar, 75
Zuppa di Cozze, *54*, 55

Editor: Michael Sand
Designer: Deb Wood
Production Managers: Denise LaCongo and Larry Pekarek

Library of Congress Control Number: 2020931055

ISBN: 978-1-4197-4763-2
eISBN: 978-1-64700-145-2

Printed and bound in the United States
10 9 8 7 6 5 4 3 2 1

ABRAMS The Art of Books
195 Broadway, New York, NY 10007
abramsbooks.com